Touchstone Skills for Authentic Communication

**Mediators Without Borders Co-Founders
Shauna M. Ries
&
Genna C. Murphy**

Published by BookLocker.com, Inc., Bradenton, Florida.

Printed in the United States of America.

BookLocker.com, Inc.
2013

First Edition

Dedication
To your authentic Self

Acknowledgements

This book is the result of a lifetime of lessons gleaned from interacting with clients and disputants and from teachers who influenced each of us along the way. We would like to begin by introducing our team of new leaders who are infusing Mediators Without Borders® with new energy and passion toward the goal of opening InAccord® Justice Centers around the United States and globally.

We would like to welcome Dan Jablonka to our advisory board and thank him for lending his extensive entrepreneurial knowledge and personal investment to the launch of the InAccord® Justice Centers. We would like to thank those seasoned professionals who have assembled to bring their expertise and advice to the Centers, including our franchise attorney Don Drysdale, franchise consultants Dennis Galloway and Michael Breidenbach, accountants Mark Carson and Deb Ziegler, and trademark attorney Will Hunziker.

This book is also the result of years of establishing systems of communication within our own organization and so we thank our faculty present and past for their help and encouragement: current instructors Brian Luther, JD and Jim Siefken. We appreciate each of you for your dedication to the field of peace making and to the success of your students.

We would also like to extend a heartfelt and grateful thank you to Dr. Susan Harter for her efforts in shaping the surveys within this volume and whose early work in authenticity and co-authorship of *In Justice, InAccord* were invaluable to this construction of this volume.

Disclaimer

This book details the author's personal experiences with and opinions about communication and working through everyday dilemmas.

The authors and publisher are providing this book and its contents on an "as is" basis and make no representations or warranties of any kind with respect to this book or its contents. The author and publisher disclaim all such representations and warranties, including for example warranties of merchantability and communication advice for a particular purpose. In addition, the author and publisher do not represent or warrant that the information accessible via this book is accurate, complete or current.

The statements made about products and services have not been evaluated by the U.S. government. Please consult with your own legal or accounting professional regarding the suggestions and recommendations made in this book.

Except as specifically stated in this book, neither the author or publisher, nor any authors, contributors, or other representatives will be liable for damages arising out of or in connection with the use of this book. This is a comprehensive limitation of liability that applies to all damages of any kind, including (without limitation) compensatory; direct, indirect or consequential damages; loss of data, income or profit; loss of or damage to property and claims of third parties.

You understand that this book is not intended as a substitute for consultation with a licensed medical, legal or accounting professional. Before you begin any change your lifestyle in any way, you will consult a licensed professional to ensure that you are doing what's best for your situation.

This book provides content related to communication and working through everyday dilemmas topics. As such, use of this book implies your acceptance of this disclaimer.

Touchstones Skills for Authentic Communication

Table of Contents

Introduction

Is This Book For You?

If you have opened this book, chances are you are interested in learning to communicate with the intention to resolve day-to-day dilemmas and build a solid foundation for what we refer to as self-liberation. By self-liberation we mean freedom from debilitating emotions, faulty cognitions and distortions in our thinking, as well as persistent patterns of miscommunication. Self-liberation occurs when you become more aware of who you are in relationship to yourself and others. You begin to understand more fully what it is to be human, with your fallibilities and misperceptions, and take another step forward to deepen your knowledge and self-awareness. You will begin to feel more comfortable revealing your true self as each component along the pathway allows you to move towards personal growth and liberation. In this book, we present a communication pathway that can lead you to a more transparent and authentic self, noting that this journey is ever a direction, replete with course corrections, integration of new perspectives, and a deepening of relationships. This pathway has, and is, making a profound difference in both the lives of those we teach and in our own personal journeys to self-liberation.

After all that has been written, studied, researched, and debated with regard to effective communication, is there anything left to learn? Moreover, if there is more to learn about communication, why this book and why now? If you are like most people, you spend a considerable amount of your time each day communicating with others. When you are not communicating with others, you are engaged in hours of self-talk, most of this occurring just outside of your awareness. What then could be more important to healthy relationships than the ongoing study and practice of healthy communication processes that lead to increased clarity and expanded liberation from self-defeating thoughts and feelings? Take a moment to answer the following inventory to see if you would benefit by incorporating the

Touchstone Skills and processes on the communication pathway into your repertoire of communication abilities.

- Would you like to learn a communication skill set based on empirical research that provides the groundwork for you to choose your own unique style of interaction?
- Is there some area in your life that would be made better if you knew how to articulate your needs more clearly?
- Do you have personal or work relationships that are confusing or difficult?
- Are there situations at work that might be helped if you had a deeper understanding of how to effectively engage in dialogue?
- Would you like to improve your ability to communicate more authentically and enhance your relationships with family and friends?
- Would you like to have a deeper level of intimacy with someone in your life?
- Are you interested in more easily building new friendships?
- Would you like to increase your self-awareness of what is driving much of your current conversations and interactions with others?
- Would you like to examine your own intra-psychic processes (your self-talk) before you speak with another person about a shared dilemma?
- Do you want to learn how to interact in a way that will liberate you and others?
- Would you like to communicate from a more positive and loving stance?

If you answered "yes" to any one of these questions, then this book can help you through a pathway of improved communication and expanded awareness of yourself and others. The stakes for better worldwide communication and cooperation are higher than they have ever been for you and for the world. Poor communication leads to misunderstandings that can mushroom into simple dilemmas or balloon into international crises. It can create tension within families and friendships, rifts that are difficult to heal and, at worst, might lead to violence in word and action. There will always be more to learn about this most fundamental human attribute of communication and we hope this book adds to your learning as you take another step forward in a larger human journey towards self-liberation.

The Touchstones Skills and Footstep Processes

At its heart, the practice of the *Touchstone Skills* addresses self-talk and interpersonal exchanges between people (be they friends, couples, or family members); within *companies* (between colleagues or between employers and employees); or in international relations (between or within countries) where issues of cultural sensitivity, compassion, and gaining perspective become all the more critical. In each case, there is an attempt to both understand and be understood by individuals and within groups. Our goal is to enable you, the reader, to share with others your own perspective in a way that aids the others in understanding who you are, what you want, and perhaps who you are seeking to become, a process we have labeled *perspective-taking/sharing/shifting*. Equally as important, you will discover what others want and need and who they are seeking to become. In this way, both perspectives are enriched and perceived differently, as we build a community one person at a time by walking a never-ending, shared pathway of increased understanding and humility.

When you begin your journey along our path, combining both the *Touchstone Skills* and the application of our *footstep processes*, you will experience a profound shift in your perceptions and gain clarity and purpose. Often times, we are lulled into dilemmas and situations that lead us down a predictable, yet undesirable path. This happens one degree at a time, as we avoid the tough conversations and deal with life habitually, out of touch with the emotional states so critical to effective communication. The resultant negative states become your indicators that you have strayed off the pathway. The *Touchstone Skills* of questioning, reflecting, and reframing, can help you find the path again by providing you with insights about how you approach a difficult situation or interpersonal challenge and the skills to move successfully through unavoidable dilemmas.

Figure 1, on the following page, presents the pathway with the six processes that are engaged after the identification of a new dilemma and end with resolution and self-liberation.

1. Revealing Emotions
2. Empowerment
3. Gaining Perspective
4. Empathy/Compassion
5. Transparency
6. Authenticity

These processes are presented in sequence, moving from revealing your emotions, to increasing your empowerment, to gaining perspective, to fostering empathy and compassion, to expanding transparency and authenticity, and, finally, to experiencing resolution and self-liberation. The *Touchstone Skills*, depicted in the middle of the circle, are the communication tools that facilitate the enactment of each of the processes that define the pathway. The skill set of questioning, reflecting, and reframing facilitates your mastery of the processes that define the journey and bring greater clarity, allowing you to move to the resolution of a given dilemma as well as to open you up to greater liberation. We are suggesting that each time you circle the pathway, you will deepen your capacity to resolve dilemmas and, in the spirit of self-liberation, enhance your understanding of your objective self. In this way, you move away from a reactionary, subjective stance to a more objective empathic awareness.

Figure 1.

A Theoretical Pathway to Self-Liberation

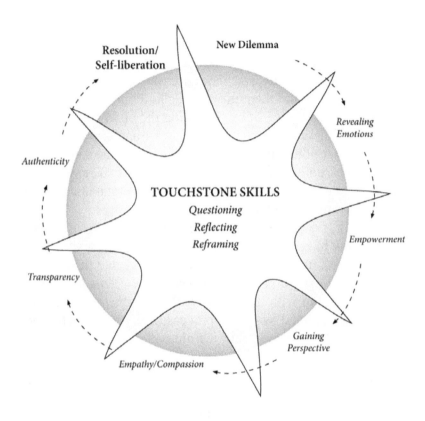

Applying the Touchstone Skills to the Circular Pathway

There are three communication skills you will be learning to practice with yourself and others as you journey along the pathway. The first of these is *questioning*, which presents inquisitive statements directed to yourself or others for the purpose of eliciting information or evoking a response. The second *Touchstone Skill* is *reflecting*, which is a process whereby you listen to your own self-talk or your dialogue with another and then mirror or echo the dialogue back either verbatim, in summarization, or by reviewing the main points. The third *Touchstone Skill* of *reframing* is a process of transforming one's own internal talk or that of another from a negative structure into one that is more easily accessed and understood. This consists of removing toxic comments and replacing them with more positive statements that are often solution-focused in intent.

In this book, we provide techniques and case scenarios designed to teach you how to apply the *Touchstone Skills* to both your self-talk and to your conversations with others. We have labeled these (1) *Intra-psychic Touchstones* and (2) *Interpersonal Touchstones*. We recommend you begin with the *Intra-psychic Touchstone Skills* as you become more acquainted with the processes along the pathway and how to use the skills to extend your learning of each one.

Footsteps along the Pathway

The skills of questioning, reflecting, and reframing can be applied to each of the six *footstep processes* along the pathway. These processes will be covered in greater detail later in the book, but for now we will offer a brief overview of each one. There will be many times that you will step back and forth between these processes, using the *Touchstone Skills* to expand your practice and understanding of the concepts as you work through each new dilemma. Your journey on the pathway begins with the identification of the new dilemma or problem to be solved.

One: Revealing Emotions. The first footstep involves identifying and understanding your emotions. Your emotions have a profound influence over your self-talk and dialogue with others; therefore, we recommend that you check the status of your emotions around a dilemma before you attempt dialogue with another.

Two: Empowerment. Empowerment is the process by which people gain mastery over issues of concern to them. The *Touchstone Skills* offer you an empowering process by providing the means to achieve not only the goal of resolving any one dilemma but the larger goal of liberating yourself from destructive patterns of behavior, thought, and emotion as you follow each footstep along the way.

Three: Gaining perspective. This is an important footstep that involves appreciating the views of self and others. The *Touchstone Skills* are invaluable tools to uncovering your own perspectives and for both uncovering and understanding the perspectives of another person.

Four: Empathy/compassion. Empathy and compassion are an extension of the process of taking in the perspectives of others, and as you apply the *Touchstone Skills*, you will see how your increased capacity for empathy occurs as you shift your perspective away from your own narrow or habituated points of view and learn to view a situation from another's vantage point. *Five: Transparency.* This footstep on the pathway begins by increasing your self-awareness and then sharing this in a candid manner. This openness, initially to yourself and then interpersonally with another, helps you engage with others in a manner that all parties can begin to rely on.

Six: Authenticity. Through the use of questioning and reflecting, you can uncover self-distortions that may blind you to your shortcomings and undermine your relationships with self and others. In this way, you begin to assess your qualities and skills with greater accuracy and learn to present your true self to yourself and others.

Resolution/Self-Liberation. Resolution refers to reaching an acceptable solution to the dilemma. Self-liberation occurs when you become more aware of who you are in relationship to yourself and others. You begin to understand more fully what it is to be human, with your fallibilities and misperceptions, and take another step forward to deepen your knowledge and self-awareness. This pathway is a never ending journey with a goal of finding ways to engage in dilemmas in a more preventative *upstream* manner before they escalate into conflicts.

Upstream Solutions

The following parable illustrates the reasoning behind our goal to encourage you to continually engage your interactions with yourself and others "upstream" rather than await a more serious situation downstream. In our quest to expand preventative measures to problem solving and decision making, we refer to a parable written by Donald B. Ardell (1977), called *Upstream/Downstream: A Contemporary Fable.* In this story, Ardell, writes about the villagers of a fictitious town called Downstream who start noticing human bodies floating past the town in the river that runs through their tiny hamlet. As the number of bodies began to increase each year, the villagers of Downstream responded admirably by continuing to rescue those they could and increase their rescue time with each passing year.

Over the years, the villagers grew proud of their expanding rescue efforts that included the new hospital at the river's edge, a flotilla of rescue boats, and highly trained personnel ready at a moment's notice to pull victims from the water. It cost the village a great deal of money, yet what else could they do when so many lives were at stake? Ardell wisely notes that few people ever questioned whether there was anything happening upstream to cause this steady increase of victims. There was just so much to do with the rescue efforts that no one had the time to investigate what was happening *Upstream.*

Ardell's fable guides our theory that many interventions into communication dilemmas occurring interpersonally, as well as across many different cultures, operate like the village of *Downstream.* Vast amounts of time and money are invested to help the victims of every imaginable conflict, health issues, and injustice yet, most people, even those interested in the cause of these health issues, crimes, and tragedies, do not direct their attention or their resources to stop the origin of the deluge *upstream.* In our previous volume, *In Justice,*

InAccord (2012), we advocated for interventions, such as mediation, as upstream endeavors that seek to help victims at the earliest point possible in any dispute. These, and many other forms of conflict resolution, including restorative justice and arbitration, can help stop the escalation of a dispute or misunderstanding before the number of casualties overwhelms the fabric of any one couple, family, community, or country.

In this book, we want to travel even further *upstream* to the point of communication breakdowns that occur before the outside experts and well-meaning professionals enter to intervene and assist couples, organizations, diplomats, politicians, and policy makers displaying differences of opinion. These are the points, often finely nuanced, where many begin to fumble in their communications, projecting false assumptions, and stepping quite inadvertently on one another's pride. These moments are the genesis of miscommunications that begin to roll downstream, picking up opponents and proponents along the way, building on initial misunderstandings and escalating into something no one *upstream* would ever have imagined. *Upstream* in this metaphor, refers to our preventative approach, encouraging a dialogue to resolve a problem situation before it turns into an acute conflict or flagrant dispute.

How the Book Unfolds

The circular pathway to self-liberation is presented in more detail through the seven chapters that follow. Our goal is to provide you with the desire to establish your personal *intention* to move along the pathway because, as Kabat-Zinn (2005) notes, "Your intentions set the stage for what is possible; they remind you from moment to moment of why you are practicing in the first place" (p. 32). Thus, we will present how important your positive attitude can be as you pay attention and listen for the differences of perspectives and perceptions with yourself and others. As you do, you will build an appreciation for how this divergent thinking can profoundly affect both your internal dialogue and the interpersonal conversations you have with others.

Additionally, the importance of being genuine and holding unconditional positive regard for others is presented as a way of developing a self-liberating pattern of communication through the practice of the *Touchstone Skills*.

Chapter One begins with a more detailed description of the *Touchstone Skills* and the *footstep processes*. This is followed by a survey where you can test yourself on your initial ability to engage in the skills of questioning, reflecting, and reframing at a general level. Several barriers to effective self-talk and interpersonal communication are introduced prior to our discussion of how to use these skills *intra-psychically* and then *interpersonally*. Specific questions and suggestions are offered for each type of skill-set (questioning, reflecting, reframing) within these two categories. We follow this discussion with a case study about a male employee and his female boss who are engaged in a workplace dilemma. The chapter ends with an exercise in which you can identify your own personal style in implementing the three *Touchstone Skills*.

Chapter Two applies the *Touchstone Skills* in practice, across a number of interpersonal contexts in which dilemmas occur in the everyday lives of individuals. We begin by applying these principles to a family case wherein a 17-year old high school senior shares his struggle with his father about whether to take time off after high school to travel or work, or go directly to college. The example takes you through the intra-psychic as well as the interpersonal skills, as each character engages in questioning, reflecting and reframing. The next case scenario is applied to a friendship dilemma where two lifelong friends struggle over the issue of spending enough time together. The final case study deals with a potential dilemma in the workplace. In each case, we trace the progress through the application of the intra-psychic *Touchstones Skills* of questioning, reflecting, and reframing as well as use of these skills on an interpersonal basis.

Chapter Three addresses both the importance of revealing and sharing one's emotions around a given dilemma as well as the important role of empowerment. Emotions, as we will discuss in this chapter, are powerful forces in human behavior. Yet they must not merely be expressed by unleashing potentially damaging displays of

10

feelings but must be acknowledged, clearly labeled, and shared in the spirit of genuine communication. Moving along the pathway, with the help of the *Touchstone Skills*, may strengthen the empowering emotions as well as diminish the experience of the disempowering emotions. Closely aligned, therefore, with the identification of where one stands in terms of these two classes of emotions, is the more general concept of empowerment in which you take a more active role in the solution of your dilemmas. In this sense, you become the leader of the journey setting up guideposts that allow you to keep your bearings along the pathway. The chapter concludes with surveys that allow you to assess your general sense of empowerment and a case study that brings together the *Touchstone Skills* and the two footsteps of revealing emotions and empowerment.

Chapter Four illustrates how gaining perspective relates to the development of empathy and compassion. Gaining perspective involves three components: understanding the perspective of others, mutually sharing your perspectives, and shifting your own perspective in the process. Each of these processes becomes critical in order to experience compassion for oneself and another, an emotional acceptance that allows you to move further along the pathway. Surveys will allow you to assess your own empathic strengths as well as your abilities to experience compassion. The chapter concludes with a case study that highlights the intersection of these two footsteps in a family case involving two parents and two adolescents deciding where to take the family vacation.

Chapter Five will first focus on the concept of transparency which, in the circle, is a precursor to authenticity. A survey to allow you to assess your own level of transparency will also be included. We then describe the journey of authenticity including barriers such as the noisy ego, faulty perceptions, and defense mechanisms. We also present ways to overcome these barriers that teach you how to quiet the noisy ego, examine internal defenses, and establish a fertile self-awareness of mindfulness and humility. This chapter concludes with self-assessment surveys designed to help you become aware of your current skills at authentic communication and a case study that will demonstrate application of the *Touchstone Skills* and how they relate to these two footsteps along the pathway.

In Chapter Six, we introduce case applications of the *Touchstone Skills* to illustrate how others might use them in non-familial context. The topics deal with bridging cultural divides along the pathway. For example, it addresses the bi-cultural adaptations to a new culture with the case of immigrants to the United States. The chapter concludes by applying the *Touchstone Skills* and *footsteps processes* to a dilemma within Constanta, Romania about what to do about packs of wild dogs that roam the streets and beaches.

In Chapter Seven of the book, we demonstrate how these skills can be integrated into the advanced practice for professional mediators, arbitrators, and those engaged in restorative justice programs, by use of the *InAccord Conflict Analysis®* model (Ries & Harter, 2012). We also provide guidelines for how to decide when it becomes too difficult to employ the various *Touchstone Skills* and the *footstep processes* on one's own, leading to the need to seek additional help. For example, we discuss when to bring in an *InAccord* mediator or arbitrator if a particular dilemma turns into a more acute conflict that requires the intervention of a third party. Additionally, we present when the assistance of an *InAccord* restorative justice facilitator would be helpful working with the victim and offender in criminal justice cases. The book concludes with a deeper discussion of the research underlying the *Touchstone Skills* and the *InAccord Conflict Analysis®* model.

Each of the six *footstep processes* presented in these chapters will be enhanced by the use of questioning, reflecting, and reframing, which allows you to more fully understand how to best communicate with others from a more authentic stance. This hopefully will prevent the development of a more acute conflict. Over time, you can actually deconstruct the habituated self, meaning that you can alter your negative ingrained patterns of behavior. There is a saying attributed to Warren Buffett that, bad habits are like chains that are too light to feel until they are too heavy to carry. The *Touchstone Skills* and the *footstep processes* will serve to facilitate this movement away from bad habits, especially those that have become too heavy to carry. Once you are able to separate yourself from your habitual thinking, you can begin to focus less on your own or another's *storyline* and more on the needs and the feelings of the storytellers.

When Ries completed her book, *In Justice, InAccord* (2012) with co-author Susan Harter, she knew there was another volume in waiting, a text that would present a more preventative narrative of how to avoid the escalation of a dilemma. In this text, we seek to address the *Touchstone Skills* necessary to deal with everyday problem-solving and decision-making situations. It is this *Touchstone Practice*, combining both the skills and theory that we offer to you, the reader. In working on this volume, we each experienced our own individual and collective transformation and it is our hope the same may happen to you along this journey. It is this combination of integration of the concepts and transformation in our dialogue that continues to loosen the grip on old ways of thinking that may longer serve us. It is our intention to personally and professionally follow the pathway to improve daily interactions and meet our overall yearning for honesty, directness, and sincerity, while maintaining and understanding the need for humility and kindness.

This book is a blend of the experiences of our fellows, advisors, teachers and graduates of Mediators Without Borders, along with the unique personal and professional experiences of each author. Shauna Ries contributes her foundation of study for her empirically proven, research based *InAccord Conflict Analysis®* model. She advances the principles of justice and injustice by addressing socio-emotional concerns through the application of her *Touchstone Skills* along with her conceptual framework for the *footstep processes* that are outlined in this book. These processes are now being evaluated to understand their influence on the quality of life for families, organizations and international institutions. Genna Murphy brings a lifetime of experience working as a therapist and coach with those in crisis. She developed curriculum for the Mediators Without Borders graduate certificate in mediation and arbitration and has had a life-long involvement in peacemaking activities. The authors are cofounders of InAccord Justice Centers, Ltd. offering franchise and InAccord Associate opportunities for graduates of the Mediators Without

Borders educational programs. Qualified graduates, with the appropriate credentials and entrepreneurial experience, will be able to submit applications for review in order to work within Centers offering mediation, arbitration, and restorative justice around the United States. In this text, each author contributes her distinct perspectives on issues involving the Touchstone processes and pathways that lead to peaceful resolutions of miscommunication and invite you to add your own insights on your own remarkable journey to self-liberation.

Chapter One
Improving Your Self-Talk and Interpersonal Communication with the Touchstone Skills

Dialogue must begin, first of all, within oneself. If we cannot make peace within, how can we hope to bring peace about in the world? -
Thich Nhat Hanh (1996)

Overview

This chapter focuses on the application of the *Touchstone Skills* to your self-talk and your dialogue with others. We begin this discussion by providing a more detailed exploration of these skills and the six footstep processes. Next, we provide you with a self-assessment wherein you can measure your skills at each skill of questioning, reflecting, and reframing. This will provide you with an understanding of your strengths and challenges in each area and allow you to focus more attention to those areas that need improvement. The self-assessment is followed by a description of how to use the three skills to understand and improve your intra-psychic self-talk including questions and techniques that can help you reveal your hidden defenses and correct faulty perceptions and thinking. Once you have a clear understanding of how to use these skills with your internal dialogue, you will learn how to apply them to conversations with others when discussing a shared dilemma or problem. Two case studies will be presented to illustrate the use of the skills both intra-psychically and interpersonally.

Applying the Touchstone Skills to the Circular Pathway

There are three communication skills you will be learning to practice with yourself and others as you journey along the pathway. The first of these is questioning, which is a grouping of words addressed to oneself or another for the purpose of eliciting information or evoking a response. There are two major categories of questions. The first are closed-ended, which refers to questions that are posed in order to elicit a "yes or "no," which may provide needed specific information. An example question might be, "When I am upset, should I wait 72 hours before having a dialogue with the other party?" The second type of questions, commonly referred to as open-ended, are structured in a manner that elicits detailed answers that can be useful to uncover more complex perceptions or to open up dialogue in a non-threatening way. For example, if you were seeking greater insight from someone to help solve an issue or deepen understanding, you might ask, "What ideas do you have about solving this dilemma?" or "Help me understand your thinking about this issue?" or, when posed to oneself "What is it about this that has me so upset?"

We will use an example of how to prepare financially for retirement in very uncertain economic times to illustrate use of the *Touchstone Skill* of questioning. Many people struggle with this issue because they do not have the monetary resources available to ensure a secure and comfortable retirement or they may possess limited or entrenched feelings about money, retirement, and savings that affect their emotional view of this dilemma. For example, you might believe that life is to be lived in the moment and have negative feelings of too much preparation because you watched one of your relatives save money in a way that seemed miserly, leading to great sadness, and only serving to make this person unhappy. However, rather than let these emotions negatively impact your actions, you can use questioning to determine if there is anything positive you can glean from this person's experience. You might then ask yourself questions such as, "Is there a way to save and not become sad and miserly?" "Can I both save money and still maintain my current lifestyle?" and

"Are there any lifestyle trade-offs I could make in order to feel more prepared to meet retirement?" In this manner, questioning helps you find greater clarity and purpose, avoiding the reactivity of those feelings and actions that have entrapped you in the past.

The second *Touchstone Skill* is reflecting, which is a process whereby you listen to your own self-talk or your dialogue with another and then restate that content back in a number of different ways. In its simplest form, reflecting involves restating the words of another or yourself verbatim, acting like a mirror that reflects back the exact words that were spoken. In more advanced applications, reflecting can be used to restate main themes of a conversation or summarize a long dialogue into a briefer statement. Regardless of the form your reflecting takes, it can have a very positive effect on your self-talk and on your understanding of the dialogue with another. It does so by helping a person who may be speaking rapidly to slow down and relax so they are more thoughtful in their conversation. Reflecting can also help someone feel that you are interested in what they are saying and value them. Finally, it can help you identify key elements of a conversation that might bring a solution to a dilemma or problem. The greater the crevasse of understanding between what you are hearing and what the other is saying, the more you will want to mirror back precisely what the other is saying. This ensures your accuracy regarding their words without your interpretation attached through inaccurate summarization.

Returning to the dilemma of saving for retirement, you have decided to sit down with your spouse or life partner to discuss this issue as it affects each of you. You tell them how you fear losing your freedom and spontaneity if you create a rigid savings plan. You explain that you do not want to end up like your relative who saved and saved and seemed so unhappy all the time. Your partner reflects back, "It sounds like you are afraid of losing your freedom and spontaneity if you stick to a rigid savings plan. You also do not want to end up like your relative who saved and saved and yet seems so unhappy all the time." As you or the other listen to personal fears echoed back, you can both feel the comfort of having another truly hear you. Additionally, you have the freedom of taking a moment to listen to your thoughts in order to determine if they are accurate and appropriate to the situation. This sets up a structure for the next process of reframing your statement.

The third *Touchstone Skill* of reframing is a process of transforming and reflecting either one's own internal talk or that of another from a negative or offensive structure into one that is more easily accessed and understood. Reframing consists of removing toxic comments that might include personal attacks, escalating statements, condescending language, ambiguity, or outright insults and replacing them with more palatable statements, usually with joint solutions in mind. Reframing often accomplishes the same objective as reflecting, yet with a greater focus on creating a conversation that does not inflame a situation and may reveal solutions. This process usually begins with a re-framing statement, such as, "It seems . . ."

In our retirement example, your partner helps you reframe your two statements to make them more solution focused. For example, she or he would reframe the first sentence to say "It sounds like your freedom and spontaneity is very important to you and you do not want to create a savings plan that diminishes either of these." The second statement would be reframed as, "It seems that your relative is very unhappy even though he saved and saved all his life. It is important to you to create a plan that makes you not only free and spontaneous but happy as well." Notice how the reframe has shifted focus from what you are afraid of to what you most value and want to retain. This can create a much safer environment for you to create a plan that honors your values and mitigates the fear responsible for inaction.

Two Applications of the Touchstone Skills

To facilitate movement along the pathway you must learn to apply the *Touchstone Skills* to both your self-talk and to your conversations with others. We have labeled these (1) *Intra-psychic Touchstones* and (2) *Interpersonal Touchstones*. We recommend you begin with the *Intra-psychic Touchstone Skills* as you become more acquainted with the processes along the pathway and how to use the skills to extend your learning of each one. *Intra-psychic Touchstone Skills* involves the use of questioning, reflecting, and reframing with your self-talk, an important precursor to entering into a dialogue with another. The *Interpersonal Touchstone Skills* involve the use of these skills in your everyday conversation with others involved in a shared dilemma.

When you apply *Intra-psychic Touchstone Skills* to your internal self-talk, you begin to engage what Deikman (1982) referred to as your *observing self*, that part of you that operates as a witness, questioning, reflecting, and reframing your dialogue in order to gain greater awareness of your motivations, interests, and defenses. You engage your observing self through questioning yourself about your role in a dilemma, engaging in self-talk, and then reflecting back the answers to find how this situation is affecting you and what unconscious thoughts or feelings might be evoked. You will continue to self-reflect and explore if there was perhaps a time when you felt this way historically that might be unduly influencing your behavior or perspective in the present. Finally you seek to redefine any negative statements into more self-liberating statements or reframes of the situation that free you to consider a different perspective.

Intra-psychic Touchstone Communication Skills

Intra-psychic refers to self-talk, first talking to yourself about the questions you have, reflecting back on these personal inquiries, and then doing an initial reframing, to the best of your ability before you engage in a dialogue with another. For example, someone sends you an email; you open it, and find an inflammatory message that attacks your personal integrity. You may have an impulse to immediately hit the "reply" key to defend yourself. However, you could take a moment to pause and reconsider and take stock of your emotional reaction by more calmly implementing intra-psychic questioning, reflecting, and reframing. First, you must take charge of controlling your emotional reactions and apply the *Touchstone Skills* to yourself.

An important element for the practice of the *Touchstone Skills* is first questioning your own thinking and then testing it in reality. You might begin this process by reminding yourself, "I am never upset for the reason I think." Indeed, most of us are never upset for the reason we think because we are constantly trying to justify our thoughts, projections and reactions as if they represent reality. Moreover, this faulty thinking builds a case to legitimize negative emotions, including righteous anger to attack others, thereby creating a world of divergent interpretations of a shared event. It can be helpful, at the outset of a dilemma or problem, to write out the story of the issue with as much clarity and calmness as possible, and address several general questions such as, "What do I really want from this situation?" "What is my life purpose, in terms of my need to be right?" and "Would I rather be right or happy?"

You can also use questioning to review past hurts or successes that might be unduly influencing your perceptions of a given situation. It is important to ask yourself meaningful questions that might reveal the reason behind your thinking. You might ask yourself the following general questions to begin to implement the skills of intra-psychic questioning. More refined examples will follow.

- "Am I justifying my thoughts in this situation by trying to make my perception the more correct point of view?"
- "Do I want to continue to defend my correctness and the thought system that separates me from another?"
- "Am I willing to let go, listen and begin to reflect on what the other is saying?"
- "What would construe success during this period of questioning for me and the other?"

This naturally leads into the next *Touchstone Skill* of reflecting, either on the issue itself or your personal interpretation, anticipating an interpersonal, reflective dialogue with another. In an actual interpersonal dialogue, you will mirror or say back what you hear the other person saying; initiating a style of reflecting that ensures you are capturing the others' sentiment accurately. However, during the intra-psychic phase, you reflect back on your own interpretation of the situation. Once you feel you have made an accurate assessment of your own reflective process, given your conscious understanding, there is now an opening for intra-psychic reframing, the third step in the *Touchstone Skills* process. In this step, you seek to envisage a common statement that may encompass and join both your concern and that of the other's in order to either make a decision or find a common solution. This process will hopefully deepen the connection between you and the other by transforming a "divide and conquer" mentality into a new shared understanding.

Sometimes, you may balk at the process of *reframing* because there is no empirical means to assess whether or not the new statement is based on another potentially inaccurate appraisal. It is true that the meaning you assign to situations outside yourself can be arbitrary. However, if appraisals and meanings ascribed to our world are only stories you tell yourself and the event in question is a mild to moderate misunderstanding, as opposed to an acute conflict, then why not reframe the story positively? In a sense, why not tell yourself a new story (perspective shifting) that enlivens you and the other instead of deepening conflict or misunderstanding? As long as the story appears reasonable or credible, it can be a powerful way to move forward in relationship and with any dilemma or problem.

Uncovering Your Internal Defenses

The successful use of the *Touchstone Skills* with another person begins with the identification of both your negative and positive emotions regarding the situation and those involved. As part of this process, you must also assess your own internal dialogue by employing skills to correct defensive thoughts, feelings, and attitudes that might work against your intention to have greater internal authenticity. This is important not only because it creates a more consistent and accurate external dialogue, but because it works to increase your level of empowering emotions. Your emotions spring from cognitive appraisals and the meaning assessments (Fredrickson, 1998) that you create; therefore, it is critical to be certain about the accuracy of these appraisals and applied meanings before acting on negative emotions and reaching for more empowering feeling states of being. One way to gain more certainty about your appraisals is to ask yourself questions that measure the accuracy of your perceptions.

There are two defense mechanisms that make the task of understanding and correcting your perceptions more difficult: *projection* and *reaction formation*. Projection is a tendency to "project" onto other people those parts of ourselves (thoughts, feelings, attitudes) that are either too unacceptable to acknowledge or exist deeply within the unconscious. An example of this is demonstrated by a husband who rails against what he insists is his wife's over dependency while constantly criticizing her for going out with her friends. In this instant, he is projecting his own dependency and fear of her leaving him, even for an evening, onto her and accusing her of being the dependent partner.

In reaction formation, anxiety often drives one's intolerable thoughts, such as racism, and provokes a response of reacting in opposition to the thoughts. In such an instance, a person might become an outspoken advocate for civil rights at the same time they are secretly involved in a hate crime. In the more benign example of this latter mechanism, a person might have a strong emotional charge about an issue and yet act completely the opposite, creating what Shakespeare referred to as a persona who "doth protest too much." In another more harmful way, we see a politician who launches an ethics investigation into corruption charges against his opponent and then is caught in a scandal that exposes his own corruption. In fact, the explanation may be that this person handled the discomfort of his own duplicity in public office, by creating an exaggerated defensive response of crusading against his opponent's same behavior in a public forum.

It is clear how these defense mechanisms and others work to create miscommunication within the individual that makes clear communication with another very difficult. Each person who seeks a more authentic way of engaging the external world must begin with an internal self-examination before speaking to the other. This awareness paves the way for the application of the *Touchstone Skills* of questioning, reflecting, and reframing. In this way, we move even further "upstream" in order to address our internal conflicts and those we have with others. In Chapter Six, we will deepen this discussion of defenses as we illustrate barriers to the footstep process of authenticity.

The practice of the *Touchstone Skills, intra-psychically,* provides additional *cool down* time to engage more clearly in a subsequent interpersonal dialogue with another person. Let's take a moment to illustrate how to use the three *Touchstone Skills* within your self-talk before trying out these tools in a conversation with another. You have already established how self-inquiry or questioning can be essential to assessing the accuracy of your perceptions of yourself and another. When applied as an intra-psychic method, questioning and reflecting become a complementary process of asking yourself questions and reflecting back both the immediate and ongoing internal responses. In a sense, you become both the reflecting mirror and the listener in this process with the added benefit of safely practicing a skill that will be applied in the future to an interpersonal dialogue with the person involved in the dilemma. The level of questioning can involve curiosity seeking of what the other person might deem as meaningful in the specific decision-making situation or it can be a deeper self-examination of what may or may not be affecting your perception in this instance.

A series of brief intra-psychic self-assessment questions might include:

- "Is this decision one that must be made quickly or can I take some time to more deeply explore my interpretation and how the other may be interpreting this situation?"
- "Am I empowered enough in this moment to make a thoughtful assessment, decision, or perception, or am I feeling reactionary?"
- "Should I wait for 72 hours to reconsider?"
- "Is this a conversation to have now, should I delay the conversation, or is the best course of action to just let it go?"

If there is a longer period of time available or the situation is complex or emotionally charged, you might ask a series of deeper questions such as:

- "Is there anything else occurring in my life right now that might be affecting how I see this situation or person?"
- "Is this situation familiar or is it something completely new to me?"
- "Does this situation or person remind me of anything or anyone else that may be affecting my ability to accurately assess the situation?"
- "Do I need more information about the person or situation in order to make a decision or engage in a conversation?"
- "What outcome do I want from this situation? What do I envisage as their desired outcome?"
- "Is my initial perception or internal reaction to this situation or person in keeping with my values?"
- "Is the other's perception of this incident perhaps in keeping with their values?"

Intra-psychic reflecting. Now that you have opened the process of questioning through self-inquiry, you can begin to note your internal responses to these questions in the form of self-talk. This can best be done by asking yourself any version of the questions provided previously and then writing down your automatic responses. Try not to engage in interpretation in the beginning but faithfully write down your instant reply to each question. For instance, let's say you are trying to decide how to reply to that hurtful email you just received. The first series of reflections provides you with a sense of the time frame within which you need to make this decision. You contemplate, "Am I empowered enough in this moment to make a thoughtful reply, or am I feeling defensive and reactionary?" Your immediate response is that you still feel emotionally charged and need to take some time to sit and reflect on this decision so you schedule some time alone to reflect.

Later that day, you retreat to a quiet place and begin to ask a series of questions to discover why this dilemma is such a struggle. You take out your journal and begin with, "What are my negative emotions regarding this email telling me?" Your immediate response may be, "I am not being respected by this person." You write down this response

24

and then ask, "Is there a way that I can reframe the situation to obtain what I need?" You may, in your reflection, decide that replying impulsively by email may just inflame the other or further confuse the issue because what you really want is respect not revenge. It may be a good time to phone this person and talk specifically about what his or her needs are. Oftentimes, emails can be confusing and easily misinterpreted and you will find that talking one-to-one may uncover the true spirit underlying the email exchange.

Intra-psychic reframing. The third tool in the practice of applying the *Touchstone Skills* intra-psychically is to identify any internal statements or frames that may be negatively impacting the situation and therefore require reframing. Reframing involves a four step process of (1) listening carefully to the statement; (2) working to understand what you or the other person's interest or message might be; (3) ignoring or removing negative language from the statement (this can often be done by simply removing any negative adverbs and adjectives from a statement); and (4) restating the message in a way that identifies any interests in more positive terms.

In the email situation, you identified that you felt insulted and disrespected by this person and respect is something you highly value. However, you know that this person matters a great deal to you and that emails can often be misinterpreted. You acknowledge that it may be important to speak directly to this person in order to understand the intentions or needs expressed in this email message. In your reframed statement, you remove the adjectives "insulted" and reframe the email as a miscommunication. Additionally, you identify two interests; (1) you want to be respected and (2) you want to maintain this relationship. Through this process, you have empowered yourself by removing negative self-references and by identifying two interests that must be resolved in order to accurately interpret and react to the situation.

Now, let us take the three tools of the *Touchstone Skills* applied intra-psychically through the following case study. A young man, Eric, is examining his decision to speak with his boss, Connie, about her lack of encouragement for his successes in the office. He begins by asking himself whether this situation reminds him of anything else and finds, using the reflection skill and writing the response in his journal, that this most certainly brings up all the times his busy mother did not acknowledge his achievements in school. Now that Eric understands he is forming his perceptions based on a past that is unchangeable, he begins to work at "reframing" his internal dialogue to more accurately reflect what is going on in the present moment. He composes several reframe statements including:

- "This situation is bringing up a lot of feelings from my relationship with my mother. It is not fair to either Connie or me to bring these charged feelings into my conversation."
- "It is not Connie's job to make me feel proud of my successes; however, I can tell her it would really help my performance if she could provide more positive feedback."
- "Expecting people to know what I need without asking is something I am working to change about myself. Here is another opportunity to tell Connie what I want and not recreate a negative event from my past."

In the next section, we will demonstrate the use of the *Touchstone Skills* interpersonally and revisit the situation of Eric and Connie as they apply the tools of questioning, reflecting and reframing to their dilemma.

The Interpersonal Touchstone Skills

The *Touchstone Skills* of questioning, reflecting, and reframing are engaged to discover the often untold *backstory* (the previously undisclosed story behind the story) of feelings and personal meanings that will certainly impact the resolution of the dilemma at hand. Once you have clarified the concerns that you bring to the situation and have become open and vulnerable about what you deem important, you are able to more openly apply questioning, reflecting, and reframing with another person who shares in this dilemma or problem. As you do this, you will begin to truly hear their backstory and the divergent personal fears, concerns, and matters of importance central to their opinions and actions. As you each listen and share your personal perspectives, the sometimes hidden personal needs can surface. At this point, these needs can be acknowledged and addressed so the dilemma might be solved in a manner that satisfies everyone involved.

As you can see from this discussion and the case scenario, the *Touchstone Skills* allow you to find a new way to open a dialogue and gain new perspectives about a given situation, either with your own internal dialogue or in conversation with others. Questioning promotes self-exploration as it challenges your own thinking and expands the possibilities that might exist just outside a fixed belief or viewpoint. Reflecting, which involves focused listening and reflection on the other party's point of view, can unveil a more empathic way of thinking about an emotionally-charged issue. When used to reveal and understand your own self-talk, reflecting becomes a direct passage to greater self-regulation, preventing reactionary first impulses that often create hurt feelings and the need for "I'm sorry." Both questioning and reflecting help to fortify this self-regulation by teaching you to pause and hold your emotional or verbal response in order to more carefully consider your intentions and desired outcome.

Reframing promotes self-liberation as it frees you to vacate your old reactionary perspective and create a space to gain a deeper understanding of the perspectives of others. Additionally, reframing invites you to expand your interpretation of a situation from a simplistic right or wrong view to one that is more holistic, embodying both your own and the other person's perspective. Finally, reframing provides an open forum for diverse ideas, helping you to combine unique perspectives into an acceptable joint-solution statement, one that is much more likely to endure. After a time of applying the *Touchstone Skills* in an intra-psychic manner, you will begin to experience more self-regulation and self-control, making it much easier for you to confront difficult situations and conversations with others. Certainly, fostering the objectivity in your perceptions and emotional state will be an invaluable precursor to authentically engaging another person in a situation that requires a thoughtful decision.

The practice of interpersonal questioning. The following list of questions will help guide you as you find which questions are most

27

comfortable for you to ask another person. Additionally, over time, you will learn that certain questions work in specific situations and with particular persons.

- "Help me understand..."
- "What do you want in this situation?"
- "What is your understanding of this situation?"
- "How can I help in this situation?"
- "What would it look like to you if this conversation ended successfully?"
- "What does this mean to you?"
- "What would help you to feel more comfortable?"
- "Educate me..."
- "I heard_____, are you saying_____?"
- "How can I help you be successful in this situation?"
- "You've told me what doesn't work for you, now what would make you more comfortable?"
- "Let me make sure I understand you. Do you want_____ or _____?"
- "How would you find the information you need to help you make this decision?"
- "Do you feel comfortable talking about this now? If not, how much time do you need before we talk about this?"

Let's return to the case of Eric and Connie; Connie asked the following open-ended questions throughout their initial conversation:

- "Eric, help me understand what you are upset about?"
- "What do you need from me that I am not providing now?"
- "What is your understanding of this situation?"
- "Is there something I can do to help make your job easier?"

Eric asked Connie:

- "Connie, how can I help you be successful in this conversation?"
- "What does my meeting my benchmarks mean to you?"
- "What would it look like for you to give me praise?"

The practice of interpersonal reflecting. Questioning naturally leads to *reflecting*, the next step in the *Touchstone Skills*. Used interpersonally, reflecting becomes a process of verbally mirroring the words of the other, back to them. It has the effect of allowing the other person to hear their own statements echoed back so they can provide feedback about the accuracy of your listening. It also helps them feel that you are making an effort to understand them and establishes a more collaborative and cordial atmosphere. Additionally, in the case of an inarticulate or shy person, reflecting can create safety and room to relax, thereby encouraging them to continue their dialogue. Mirroring helps the other person to hear what they said and clarify their own thinking.

Reflecting is a fundamental *Touchstone Communication Skill* that takes time to learn to use effectively; therefore, at first, it is advisable to mirror the content of what the other has communicated, almost verbatim. If the other person is uncomfortable at hearing their words mirrored back in this way, you can reassure them that your intention is to make sure that you understand clearly their intent. Many times, a person, particularly under stress, will talk rapidly and repeat phrases unknowingly. The process of mirroring back the words can help them slow down, in an attempt to underscore the importance of their utterance. In effect, once they feel you have actually heard them, they can move on to another point, and become clearer about their intentions.

At first, your practice of reflecting may seem stilted or awkward, yet the positive effects it has on a conversation can be transformational. It is best to try this out with someone you know such as a colleague or family member who understands that it is a *Touchstone Skill*. With time, it can be applied to less familiar people and situations and interspersed with the more advanced type of reflecting referred to as paraphrasing or summarizing. Using this type of reflecting, you listen for the basic message in terms of content, feeling, and meaning and then reflect the message back in much fewer words than originally used. Because this involves more practice and therefore more likelihood of mistakes, it is helpful to begin the statement with, "Let me see if I understand what you are saying. . ." and end with ". . . is that correct?"

Whether the technique used is mirroring or summarizing, it is important to be natural and restate what you have been told in the simplest of terms. Reflecting is employed to ensure that you are hearing the other person's message accurately; therefore, it is also important to avoid asking unnecessary questions, adding to the other's meaning, taking the other into a direction they did not intend, or unintentionally asserting too much control or judgment with the other's content. In the beginning, it is recommended to use some standard opening statements when summarizing another's speech. The following are taken from *In Justice, InAccord* (Ries & Harter, 2012) for use in mediation but can be adapted for any interpersonal situation.

- "One theme you keep coming back to seems to be. . ."
- "Are you okay if I try to recap the ground we have covered so far . . ."
- "I've been thinking about what you've said. Let me see if I have this right . . ."
- "As I've been listening to you, your main concern seems to be . . ."
- "I think I just heard you say. . ."

Eric and Connie Revisited. Earlier, Connie had questioned Eric, "Help me understand what you are upset about?" Eric had taken time to understand how his mother's rejection was influencing his reaction so he was able to calmly ask for what he needed, "Connie, it would really help if you could provide more feedback on my success." To reflect accurately back, Connie might say, "I hear you say that it is important to have more feedback on your success, is that correct? Let me tell you about some accomplishments and benchmarks I have noted about you over the years." Reflecting will now set up a bridge to reframing the dilemma with the solution in mind.

The practice of interpersonal reframing. It is important to remember that reframing helps to shift perspectives and therefore changes how people conceptualize their attitudes, behaviors, issues, and interests. The skill of restating the structure of a situation in a way

30

that accurately reflects the content makes it easier for all those involved in a conversation to listen to each other. Thus, reflecting paves the way for productive reframing. Remember, that in reframing the insults, personal attacks, escalating statements, condescending put-downs, ambiguity and negative over-generalizations are softened or even eliminated. Reframing often compliments the objectives of reframing. You reflect back the content of the other person's message, typically in a way that makes the message more easily heard by the other.

Yet, there is an important subtle difference between reflecting and reframing. Reflecting actually unites you with the other person, because it begins with a statement such as, "You think . . ." or "You feel . . ." and mirrors or summarizes what the other person said. Reframing builds on this deepening understanding of the other and helps shift the perception by framing statements in more positive and solution-focused ways. In a sense, reframing begins the process of taking in another person's perspective and then helping him or her shift it in order to create solutions. It is this shift to a win-win situation that is the hallmark of reframing.

Survey on the Touchstone Skills

To enhance your understanding of the skills of questioning, reflecting, and reframing and allow you to think about how they operate in your own life, we have written the survey below. It is important to remember that there are no right or wrong answers, the survey is simply designed to allow you to express your own opinions. People differ in terms of the relative value they place on these skills and whether they enhance or possibly interfere with relationships. People also differ on their ability to enact such skills.

There are three subscales for the three skills of questioning, reflecting, and reframing. For each separate skill subscale, there are six items. You may wish to add up your scores for individual items (where the item scores are given after each response choice you checked, from 4 to 1.) After you calculate this total, then divide by six in order to obtain your overall average score for each skill subscale that can range from 4 to 1. The higher scores mean that you value a given skill; the lower scores mean that you question its value or find it challenging to employ in your own relationships.

Touchstone Skills Survey. This survey asks questions about your attitudes and own experiences in employing the *Touchstone Skills* in your communications. Please review each statement below and choose **ONLY ONE RESPONSE FROM THE FOUR**. If you feel that two responses might apply, please decide on which one *is TRUER for you.* Do not check in between the words.

QUESTIONING SKILLS

1. It seems that in a close relationship, it is healthy to question the other's perspective, as well as one's own, to bring clarity to both people.

☐ Very true (4) ☐ Sort of true (3) ☐ Not very true (2) ☐ Not at ALL true (1)

2. When an issue arises in a relationship, I find it hard to realistically question my own perspective or the other person's point of view, it is easier to just leave things as they stand.

☐ Very true (1) ☐ Sort of true (2) ☐ Not very true (3) ☐ Not at ALL true (4)

3. Some things are not to be questioned in a relationship; you just go with the other person's perspective so as not to cause friction.

☐ Very true (1) ☐ Sort of true (2) ☐ Not very true (3) ☐ Not at ALL true (4)

4. Questioning perspectives in a relationship can be healthy, if one can do so in a manner that can truly be heard.

☐ Very true (4) ☐ Sort of true (3) ☐ Not very true (2) ☐ Not at ALL true (1)

5. Directly asking someone to clarify his/her point of view can positively influence a relationship.

☐ Very true (4) ☐ Sort of true (3) ☐ Not very true (2) ☐ Not at ALL true (1)

6. People have a right to their own viewpoint, so it is best not to question my own perspective or challenge the other person's, in a close relationship.

☐ Very true (1) ☐ Sort of true (2) ☐ Not very true (3) ☐ Not at ALL true (4)

SUM OF SIX ITEM SCORES = _____ DIVIDE BY SIX TO GET AVERAGE SCORE OF _____

REFLECTING/LISTENING SKILLS

1. Reflecting back on another person's perspective is hard for me because I typically think that my own perspective is usually more correct.

☐ Very true (1) ☐ Sort of true (2) ☐ Not very true (3) ☐ Not at ALL true (4)

2. Part of a good relationship is listening and then reflecting back what you have heard the other person say.

☐ Very true (4) ☐ Sort of true (3) ☐ Not very true (2) ☐ Not at ALL true (1)

3. I try hard to carefully listen and then reflect back what I think I heard the other person say, although it is admittedly sometimes a challenge.

☐ Very true (4) ☐ Sort of true (3) ☐ Not very true (2) ☐ Not at ALL true (1)

4. In a close relationship, listening and reflecting back on the other person's perspective, if we differ, is difficult for me because I trust my own instincts.

☐ Very true (1) ☐ Sort of true (2) ☐ Not very true (3) ☐ Not at ALL true (4)

5. I want to share my understanding of another person's perspective and then tell them what I have heard, but want to develop better skills to facilitate this goal.

☐ Very true (4) ☐ Sort of true (3) ☐ Not very true (2) ☐ Not at ALL true (1)

6. Often I find that I listen to the other person's point of view with a "deaf ear" and don't reflect back my understanding of what he/she thinks or feels.

☐ Very true (1) ☐ Sort of true (2) ☐ Not very true (3) ☐ Not at ALL true (4)

SUM OF SIX ITEM SCORES, DIVIDE BY SIX TO GET AVERAGE SCORE _____

REFRAMING SKILLS

1. I see the value of reconsidering or reframing my point of view in a close relationship; although challenging, it is often helpful to think "outside of the box."

☐ Very true (4) ☐ Sort of true (3) ☐ Not very true (2) ☐ Not at ALL true (1)

2. Altering one's personal frame of reference about an issue can be beneficial in a close relationship, in order to consider things in a different light.

☐ Very true (4) ☐ Sort of true (3) ☐ Not very true (2) ☐ Not at ALL true (1)

3. We come into relationships asking people to accept us as we are; we should not be expected to change our view or attitudes.

☐ Very true (1) ☐ Sort of true (2) ☐ Not very true (3) ☐ Not at ALL true (4)

4. We should enter into close relationships with like-minded people who think just the way we do, so we do not have to change our ways of framing issues or our attitudes.

☐ Very true (1) ☐ Sort of true (2) ☐ Not very true (3) ☐ Not at ALL true (4)

5. Reframing or altering one's personal views in a close relationship can be eye-opening. We can get too locked into our own perceptions, in ways which may be limiting.

☐ Very true (4) ☐ Sort of true (3) ☐ Not very true (2) ☐ Not at ALL true (1)

6. It is important to express one's convictions in a close relationship and to not be expected to challenge one's ways of thinking that can be too disruptive.

☐ Very true (1) ☐ Sort of true (2) ☐ Not very true (3) ☐ Not at ALL true (4)

SUM OF THE SIX ITEM SCORES =_____ DIVIDE BY 6, FOR YOUR AVERAGE SCORE_____

Once you have tabulated your scores, write them down in a journal or notebook. Then, after you have completed reading this text, take the survey again to see if you have experienced any movement or improvement in the survey with regard to each skill.

Assessing Your Touchstone Skills Communication Style

Table 1, Differing Styles of Communication in Approaching the Touchstone Skills, identifies the three intra-psychic skills of questioning, reflecting and reframing and the three interpersonal skills of questioning, reflecting, and reframing. For each *skill*, first identify whether you are more like the person described on the left or the right, **in the bold type.** Note that underneath each description listed in bold, there is a suggestion for how to expand your ability with this skill. Once again, keep your answers in a notebook and see if there has been a shift in your style after reading this book and practicing the *Touchstone Skills.*

35

Table 1. Different Styles of Communication in Approaching the Touchstone Skills

RECOGNIZING COMMUNICATION CHALLENGES	RECOGNIZING COMMUNICATION STRENGTHS
Intra-psychic (self-talk): Questioning Skills	
I display more negative, disempowering emotions, which can be destructive in a relationship. Be prepared to take time to *reflect* on how to *reframe* your negative feeling to a more positive emotion before sharing with another. Your negative emotions may be an indicator to evaluate your current relationship and explore options *you might do* to *reframe perspectives.*	**I usually display the more positive, empowering emotions, but this can make it more difficult for the other person in a relationship.** It is often times helpful to *match* the feeling of the other, and then gradually lean back; a good leading question might be *"have you thought about..."* and mention a slightly higher emotion on our emotional scale.
It is hard for me to formulate questions on my own, to identify what I should focus on. It is confusing to me and I don't know how this will help me in a relationship. Intra-psychic questioning allows you time to consider more deeply how you are impacted by a situation and may reveal answers that will lead you to better decision making and problem solving with another. It also gives you a moment to pause before automatically reacting.	**I can see the value of first talking to myself about what I see are possible roadblocks and to ask myself questions that help clarify my thinking. But then what do I do with the information?** Every situation or dilemma you face can be assisted by more information about your motives, your intentions, and what you are ultimately seeking in resolution or change. This will give you a more authentic bearing in your dialogue with others.

Intra-psychic (self-talk): Reflecting Skills	
I cannot imagine myself repeating back my thoughts and feelings. To what end? What could I possible learn by parroting back my own answers and emotions. Intra-psychic reflecting allows you to state out loud or silently to yourself what you are thinking and feeling internally. Often, these thoughts and feelings exist just outside our conscious awareness and reflecting on the situation or dilemma can bring these to the surface. Better to know ahead of time instead of being overwhelmed or tripped up by them.	**I can see how it could be helpful to try to at least understand my own emotions and thoughts that are linked to this situation. But how would it actually help me in my dialogue with the other person?** Reflecting on your thinking and feeling before you begin a conversation with another, prepares you to know what you want, what you do not want, and why. It can also help you understand if strong emotions come to the surface during the dialogue.
Intra-psychic (self-talk): Reframing Skills	
I can begin to see why questioning and reflecting can help me clarify my feelings and thoughts ahead of any interactions with others involved in the situation. However, what possible good could come of restating anything in a more positive manner. Intra-psychic reframing is a practice that can not only improve your dialogue with others but your inner dialogue as well. Over time, you will begin to notice negative thinking and replace it with a more positive statement called a reframe. This also gives you invaluable practice before you try reframing with another person.	**Reframing seems like a great tool to bring greater harmony to my inner dialogue. How can I effectively pose a reframe to myself?** Reframing is similar to replacing negative self-talk with positive affirmations. However, it is even more nuanced in that it takes the actual negative talk and reworks the wording into more constructive inner dialogue. Each time you do this, you will be replacing habitual negative conversations with intentional positive self-talk.

Interpersonal Questioning Skills	
I find it difficult to question or challenge another's viewpoint, they have a right to their own perspective, and it avoids friction. The act of questioning is more about curiosity versus a challenge. It allows for more compassion and understanding of the other.	**It is healthy to question the other's perspective; it brings clarity to each person in the relationship, although when I try, I don't feel that my skills are finely tuned.** It helps to begin with questions such as *"Help me understand..."* This creates an opening versus a *why* question, which may leave the other defended and guarded.
Interpersonal Reflecting Skills	
Reflecting back another person's perspective is difficult for me because I often just instinctively think my own perspective is more accurate. The greater the crevasse between perspectives in a relationship, the more important it is to say precisely back what you just heard. For instance, begin with *"you feel that you..."* and then repeat verbatim what that person is saying.	**I try to share my understanding of the other person's' point of view, to listen and tell them what I have heard, but could develop further skills to facilitate this goal.** One of the most rewarding qualities in a relationship is to be with someone who truly listens. It has been said we have two ears and one mouth to listen twice as much as we speak.

Reframing Skills in a Relationship	
I tend to come into relationships and expect people to accept me as I am. Then, we don't have to change our thinking or reframe the issues. Personal growth comes when we explore our differing perspectives. This does not mean agreement, rather a willingness to move from a fixed position and begin to listen and reflect. As a result your relationship will deepen as you frame old divisive perspectives into more inclusionary statements.	**Altering or reframing my point of view about an issue can be very valuable in a relationship, in order to consider things in a different light. This is challenging for me to do, because it does not come naturally.** Reframing issues and topics is a critical skillset that requires a blending of reflecting both on the others' and your own thoughts and feelings. This directly reduces anxiety and tension and creates a sense that you are in this together. It is a wonderful talent worth nurturing.

Defining the Footsteps along the Pathway

The skills of questioning, reflecting, and reframing can be applied to each of the six *footstep processes* along the Touchstones Pathway. There will be many times that you will step back and forth between these processes, using the *Touchstone Skills* to expand your practice and understanding of each concept as you work through each new dilemma. Your journey on the pathway begins with the identification of the new dilemma or problem to be solved. In many cases, this new dilemma will cause minimal discomfort and be transitory in nature. As such, you will find that you often move quickly through the pathway to address and resolve minor dilemmas. However, some dilemmas will be more persistent and require multiple trips along the pathway with each journey deepening your understanding and ability to navigate the dilemma more easily the next time. Our team at *Mediators Without Borders* began to note that when we were individually or collectively faced with a new dilemma or problem to be solved, it was important to begin each journey with the realization and acceptance that stories often diverge around a given situation. This has helped us develop more measured responses and solutions and sets a tone of openness to new ideas, opinions, and solutions.

Revealing Emotions. The next footstep involves identifying and understanding your emotions. Here, the application of the *Touchstone Skills* can facilitation this comprehension, both within you and with others. Your emotions have a profound influence over how you converse, how you deal with problems, and how open you are to differences of opinion and perspective. Yet, many times you may engage in conversations or dive immediately into a dilemma without first checking your emotional barometers. Ries and Harter (2012) have presented a strong case for the importance of the role of emotions in mediation and other forms of conflict resolution. Ries developed a conceptualization of two types of emotions in a given case, those which are empowering, such as hope and optimism, and emotions that are disempowering, such as depression, humiliation and despair.

Ries and Harter's research has revealed that increasing the intensity of empowering emotions and decreasing the intensity of disempowering emotions is more likely to resolve issues that emerge in conflicts. Ries' premise is that it is vital to know the emotional state of people in conflict in order to know the best approach to use in each mediation case. Those with similar emotional states, meaning both individuals were empowered or both individuals were disempowered, could sit at a table and actually discuss the situation together with the mediator. On the other hand, when there was a mismatch of emotions, meaning one individual was empowered and the other disempowered, it was best to keep these individuals in separate rooms with the mediator shuttling back and forth to assist the disputants with perspective-taking, sharing, and shifting until the disputants could bring their emotional states into more balance with one another.

The process of revealing and understanding emotions is just as critical in less conflicted situations. If you know your emotional state around a given situation, you will be better prepared to take time to examine whether the emotions are appropriate to the situation or out of proportion. If the latter is the case, you can use the *Touchstone Skills* to deepen your understanding of your emotional response and enter a conversation more balanced and measured. Understanding your emotions can also help you determine if there is a mismatch between the emotions of anyone involved in the dilemma. For instance, you may feel disempowered by the situation as determined by your feelings of anger or despair, whereas the other person feels hopefulness and optimism. Rather than rushing in with your anger, you might take some time to ask them why they feel hopeful. Hearing their more hopeful perspective might help you move from negative to more positive emotions and be better able to engage in a mutual solution. This emotional shift from disempowering emotions to more empowering ones provides a springboard to move to the next process of *empowerment*.

    Empowerment: Confidence in ability to resolve the dilemma. Empowerment is the process by which people gain mastery over issues of concern to them. Rappaport (1987) noted that people gain empowerment when they are given the opportunity to "control their own destiny and influence the decisions that affect their lives" (p.119). He went on to state that an empowering process allows people to envision a closer connection between their goals and how to achieve them and affords them greater access to resources that help them gain mastery in their own lives. The *Touchstone Skills* offer you an empowering process by providing the means to achieve not only the goal of resolving any one dilemma but the larger goal of liberating yourself from destructive patterns of behavior, thought, and emotion as you follow each footstep along the way.

    The process of empowerment begins when you first identify your emotions and understand how they are affecting your perspective in a given situation. As you learn to move away from negative feelings to more empowering emotions, you gain greater confidence in your ability to master your own life rather than be driven by forces that you can neither identify nor control. Revealing your emotions sets the stage for a deeper examination of your goals and what means you have at your disposal to realize these goals. The *Touchstone Skills* used both intra-psychically and interpersonally, open up a greater reservoir of hope by expanding the options available both within hidden areas of your own self and through hearing the options of another. As we take the time to understand ourselves and the other, we begin to broaden our perspective by expanding what we can tolerate internally and by accepting the view of another even when it differs dramatically from our own.

Gaining perspective. This is an important footstep that involves appreciating the views of self and others. By now, you are expanding your understanding of how much of your perspective comes from your individual history and experiences, both positive and negative. When caught in a dilemma, you may unconsciously revert back to the past and evoke memories of pleasurable or painful events that now influence your current decisions. Perspectives can be thought of spatially, using the metaphor of mountain climbing. If you approach a mountain from the east, it will be a very different experience than scaling it from the west. The same is true with your psychological perspectives, especially when faced with a challenging situation. One person's perception may not match the experience of another, much like scaling the mountain from different directions. However, by activating the observing self, you can expand old perceptions and help everyone involved in the situation gain a deeper acceptance and appreciation of the unique perspectives of the others. The *Touchstone Skills* are invaluable tools to uncovering your own perspectives and for both uncovering and understanding the perspective of another person. Through the empowering process of asking thoughtful questions, reflecting back with understanding, and taking time to carefully reframe destructive comments and internal thoughts, you begin to move along a continuum of sharing and shifting perspective. This important process sets the stage for the next process of deepening empathy and evoking compassion for oneself and for others.

Empathy/compassion. Empathy and compassion are an extension of the process of taking in the perspectives of others, a process that demonstrates understanding and connection. Empathy is defined in many different ways according to the field of study that seeks to define and measure it. Researcher Batson (2009) placed these many definitions into eight distinct concepts. Our definition of empathy aligns with Batson's concept of this as the ability or process of imagining how another person is thinking and feeling. Batson noted that empathy "is measured by ones' sensitivity to the way the other is affected by his or her situation" (p.7). Batson notes that Barrett-Lennard (1981) referred to this as adopting an "empathic attentional set" that involves "a process of feeling into, in which Person A opens him-or herself- in a deeply responsive way to Person B's feelings and experiencing but without losing awareness that B is a distinct other self" (p. 92). This particular conceptualization of empathy is referred to by Stotland (1969) as a form of perspective taking where you "imagine" the other's thoughts and feelings.

With practice, you will see how your increased capacity for empathy occurs as you shift your perspective away from your own narrow or habituated points of view and learn to view a situation from another's vantage point. In a sense, gaining perspective and increasing empathy go hand in hand, each one expanding as you deepen the other. We define *compassion* as the deeper emotional component to this process, where your awareness shifts to a more expansive desire to alleviate another person's suffering. The Dalai Lama (Lama & Cutler, 1998) defines compassion as, "a state of mind that is non-violent, non-harming, and non-aggressive. . . based on the wish for others to be free of their suffering" (p. 89) He also points out that the development of compassion begins with the wish that oneself be free of suffering and from this expanded state it is extended out to the other. This is in keeping with our recommendation that you first apply the *Touchstone Skills* to your own self and then to others. Once you have established a strong understanding of yourself, it is easier to share this with another rather than hide your thoughts and feelings from them. This is the foundation for the next footstep of *transparency*.

Transparency. This footstep on the pathway indicates your personal intention to openly dialogue with another. It begins by increasing your self-awareness and clarifying your own perspective. This openness, initially to yourself and then interpersonally with another, helps you engage with others in a manner that all parties can begin to rely on. Indeed, this commitment to openness can build trust with the other person even though your perspectives and values may differ. We have discussed how the *Touchstone Skills* used intra-psychically can help you increase your self-awareness of hidden motivations and defenses and activate your observing self. The process of transparency helps you expand those thoughts, feelings, and ideas that exist just outside your everyday awareness. Over time, you will increase your comfort with these thoughts and feelings as they arise. With this increased comfort, you become more at ease with who you are and what you are willing to share with another. In most of the literature and research, transparency is characterized as an essential element that serves the next footstep of *authenticity*; you need to become transparent before you can truly adopt an authentic stance. Throughout this book, you will discover how these two principles build upon one another.

Authenticity. In this book, we present Harter's (2012) concept of the authentic self to the process of communication and relate it to our ability to become vulnerable and transparently open as we develop and apply the questioning, reflecting, and reframing skills. One feature of authenticity is the development of interpersonal interactions that are real and genuine, that reflect each person's true self, what Martin Buber (1970) refers to as *I and Thou* relationships. As will become apparent, the *Touchstone Skills* and *footstep processes* will each assist you in uncovering this true nature, or authentic self, by exploring the thoughts, as well as the personal meanings you attach to these thoughts, when you are engaged in a dialogue that exposes a difference in values or opinions. Personal authenticity was described as an essential component of the mediation process in Ries and Harter's book, *In Justice, InAccord.* Authenticity, in this setting occurs when the mediator and the disputants identify and communicate their true interests, their underlying thoughts and emotions. The authors believe that an authentic and transparent trade of information can better move disputants toward a sustainable, negotiated, settlement (Ries & Harter, 2012, p. 54).

Personal authenticity is essential, not only in disputes that require professional assistance such as mediation, but just as importantly in the typical dilemmas that you encounter each and every day. Leary (2004), a prominent social psychologist notes that egocentric self-distortions can blind us to our shortcomings and undermine our relationships with self and others. Over time, we may come to believe that these distortions are authentic and take them into our relationships with others. Harter (2012) underscores this by observing that these self-distortions can also contribute to misunderstanding and mismanagement of the struggles and dilemmas that confront us in our daily lives. The *Touchstone Skills* will help you uncover your self-distortions through accurate self-questioning and reflection. You will find your ability to be authentically expanded, as your understanding of yourself and others help you avoid faulty conclusions that can lead to faulty decision-making and problem-solving. This will help you move more effortlessly toward the end goals of a resolution of the dilemma and self-liberation, a topic to which we now return.

Resolution/Self-Liberation: The Culmination of the Pathway. At the end of your journey through the pathway, you will reach a point of resolution and increased self-liberation. As we mentioned in the introduction, this liberation is marked by a growing awareness of who you are in relationship to yourself and others. It comes as a result of learning to recognize your fallibilities and misperceptions and applying skills that liberate you from habitually negative patterns of self-talk and interpersonal dialogue. Every time you commit to journeying along this pathway, you will acquire confidence that carries into the next dilemma, ever expanding your abilities, understanding, and connection with others. In this way, you increase your value to both yourself and others. As Albert Einstein once noted, your true value as a human being can be found in the degree to which you have attained liberation from the self. In the next chapter, we will help you deepen your understanding of the pathway by applying the *Touchstone Skills* to three different case scenarios involving a family, a friendship, and a workplace relationship.

Chapter Two
The Touchstone Communication Skills in Practice

Overview

At this point, you have taken a self-assessment that demonstrates your strengths and challenges with regard to each of the three *Touchstone Skills*. Now that you are beginning to understand the aims of each skill and to learn specific techniques to apply them, we will deepen this understanding by providing case scenarios that take you through the application of the three skills to interpersonal life situations that involve decision-making and problem-solving. In this chapter, we will illustrate these processes in cases involving family, friends, and co-workers. We will first highlight the importance of initially identifying emotions, the first of the six footsteps on the pathway. Once the emotions underlying the scenario are revealed, you will see how the *Touchstone Skills* of questioning, reflecting, and reframing, can be used in the service of people desiring to reach an agreeable solution.

As we mentioned in the introduction, a central theme along the path to self-liberation is to first identify and label emotions, some of which may be empowering, such as happiness and optimism, and some of which may be disempowering, such as depression, humiliation, or despair, with an eye toward increasing the intensity of the more positive emotions and decreasing the intensity of the more negative emotions. In Chapter Three, we examine this footstep of revealing emotions along with the footstep of empowerment in much more depth; however, we will apply the first of these steps to the cases presented in this chapter because it is an important precursor to using the *Touchstone Skills* effectively.

Using the Touchstone Skills in Families: Trevor's Dilemma

The following case study illustrates the combination of intrapsychic and interpersonal uses of the *Touchstone Skills*. Trevor, a 17-year-old high school senior, is trying to decide between going to college next year or taking a year off to travel and work. Trevor confided his struggle with this decision to his father who offered to help Trevor problem solve this issue over the coming weekend. In the meantime, Trevor decides to continue journaling about the issue to refine what interests he might have and work to remove any negative self-references. His father also arranged some time alone where he could prepare for the conversation by examining his motives and concerns about Trevor's choice.

Trevor's intra-psychic questioning and reflecting. Trevor had been mulling this decision over for some time now and committed to using his journal to deepen this process by going through the steps of questioning, reflecting, and reframing. He began by asking himself when this decision had to be made. His immediate reflection was, "Yesterday, dude! Stop procrastinating!" Next, he asked what information he needed to help guide his decision. He noted that he wanted to know what each decision would cost him in the future and how his friends and family might react to either choice. Reflecting, he used the word "slacker" if he chose not to go to college and that this would make him a disappointment to his parents and teachers. He asked if there was anything looming over this decision that was making it more difficult. Trevor immediately thought of his basketball coach who was pushing him to take advantage of a partial scholarship to a great regional school. He was afraid of losing the coach's respect and friendship if he not only did not take the scholarship but did not play basketball at all at the college level.

Trevor's reframing. Trevor wrote down three major statements that he made that he most wanted to change. The first was, "This is driving me crazy, and I need to make this decision now. It should not take me this long to figure this out." He reframed this as, "This is a life

48

decision I am making that will affect me and a lot of other people so of course it is taking a long time. I don't need to have a final decision for thirty more days. It is worth taking this time to be sure." The second reframe was of the statement, "Mom and Dad are going to be disappointed in me if I don't go right on to college. My friends will think I am a big loser and slacker, and so will I on some level." He reframed this as, "I am worried about other people's reactions to my choice, especially if I choose to take a year off. But, Mom always tells me that we cannot live our lives according to what other people want. Only I can know what is best for me." The final statement was, "Coach Hayes will lose respect for me if I don't take his advice. He worked so hard to help me improve as a player and I don't want to let him down." His reframe was, "I am grateful to Coach Hayes for making me a better player and I respect his advice. It may be that he will not care that much if I don't play in college."

The father's intra-psychic questioning and reflecting. Trevor's father recognized that this choice was bringing up memories of his own struggles in high school to decide what to do next. He asked himself some pointed questions about Trevor's situation so he could be more helpful. He asked himself what about this situation most reminded him of his similar situation. His immediate response was that he was never really sure that the decision he made back then was the right one. His next question was how he could help Trevor be successful in resolving this issue. He noted that he was afraid he would influence him in order to make up for the decision he made all those years ago.

The father's reframing. Next, he decided to take the two statements that were most negative and reframe them into positive, affirming assertions. He was surprised to find one statement as, "I want to make sure Trevor does the right thing but I'm afraid I'll screw up and force him to make a choice he will regret." He reframed this as, "Only Trevor knows what is right for Trevor. He is a smart, capable young man and I trust him. I won't force anything on him as long as I just listen carefully and help him help himself." His other statement had to do with his own decision in high school, "I regret that I ever went on to play football in college and ruined my knee for life. Dad was such a jerk when I was in this situation. He treated me with contempt and tried to live out his failed football career through me. I will never do that with Trevor." His reframe softened this statement to, "I loved playing football in college and made lifelong friends on that team. I could have just as easily hurt my knee skiing or running as a young man. And, dad only did what he thought was best for me. Every generation gets better at guiding their kids, and I know I will do better by giving Trevor the encouragement my father gave without the pressure and undue influence."

Interpersonal questioning. His father began their meeting by asking him, "How can I help?" This simple yet powerful question allowed Trevor the freedom to have control of how the decision making process would be set up. Trevor responded that he would like to have his help in making the decision but without any direct advice. His father then asked him, "What are some of the "do's and don'ts" you want from me in terms of helping you?" Trevor responded that he would like help uncovering anything he might be overlooking or anything that he might be unaware of that was influencing his decision. Trevor told his father he wanted to ask him questions, as well, about his former college experiences.

His father asked Trevor, "What are the opportunities and challenges of going to college next fall?" Trevor responds by stating, "I worked so hard in high school to maintain my GPA, letter in four sports, and do all these activities to get into the best school. Now, I have the chance to go anywhere I want and I just feel burned out." His father then asked, "Are there any pressures that you feel right now that are influencing you to go to college?" Trevor shared his fears about disappointing his father and mother and his coach. His father then asked him, "What are the opportunities and challenges of taking a year off before college?" Trevor then asked his father the following questions, "Dad, how did you decide whether to go to college or not?" "Do you ever regret that decision?" "What do you wish you had done differently?"

Interpersonal reflecting. Trevor's father reflected back Trevor's initial statement as, "It seems you are worried that you have worked so hard to get into these colleges that you might be too burned out to actually go?" Trevor nods to his father and adds, "Dad, I won't make it. I am so afraid I will fail." Because his father was willing to just reflect and not advise, Trevor was able to quickly move to his underlying fears of failure. His father then reflected back his concerns about other people being disappointed, "It seems like you are fearful of disappointing your mother and me and Coach Hayes." Trevor had spoken for some time about the challenges and opportunities of taking a year off so his father summarized in order to hit the key phrases and points. "Trevor, it sounds like taking a year off would allow you more time to know what you want to do with your life. It sounds like you hope it will allow you to rest and be better prepared when you finally do go. However, you are also worried that you will lose momentum by stopping your education, and you are terrified that you will never go to college and end up working in a low paying job."

Trevor took some time to reflect back his father's answers to his questions. In the first instance he mirrored it back almost verbatim, "It sounds like you never really consciously decided to go to college. It was expected of you and so you did it." In the second instance, his father had talked about some regrets he had and how he had reflected on those and made peace by focusing on the positive things that came from playing football in college. Trevor reflected back, "So, you do have regrets, especially about tearing up your knee. But, you also appreciate the great friends you made along the way." His father had taken a bit longer to respond to what he would have done differently so Trevor summarized what he heard to this point, "What I hear you saying is that you don't know if you would have made a different decision but it would have helped if you had taken the time to be sure. Sounds like grandpa really pressured you so that you never quite knew if you were doing it for him or for yourself."

Interpersonal Reframing. At this point, Trevor's father reframed the situation by removing the toxic language and stating the content in a solution focused account. "Trevor, it sounds like you really applied yourself in high school so you could get into the best schools and you did. Now, you are tired and worn out and worried that this might affect your performance at college." At this point, he added a problem solving statement, "It sounds like you need to do something that will help you feel refreshed and ready when college starts. Right now, you have one idea to remedy that which is taking a year off." This reframe and problem solving statement, allowed Trevor to break free from the dead-end statement of failure, be reminded how he succeeded in high school to get what he wanted, and open up the idea that taking a year off may be just one idea that solves this dilemma. This conversation continued over several weeks until Trevor, without any perceived pressure or advice from his father, was able to find two solutions: 1) take 30 days prior to college completely off to go on a couple of fishing trips in Canada; and 2) not commit to any extracurricular activities or sports his freshman year.

This is one example of how to apply the *Touchstone Skills* to a problem-solving circumstance between parent and teen. In reality, this conversation would have been much more fluid with the three skills interwoven within the conversation; however, it is easier to learn new skills by thinking of them first in a linear manner. After a time using them in real situations, you will begin to apply them in more nuanced ways, weaving the skills together rather than building one upon the other.

Using the Touchstone Skills in a Friendship

In this next scenario, Carson and Lee, childhood friends, are facing a dilemma about how and when to spend time together. Lee is a busy psychotherapist, spends 50 hours a week in individual and group sessions, and by Friday afternoon each week, is in need of quiet time and rest. Carson is a website designer and spends a great deal of time working from her home office, creating websites and only occasionally speaking with clients via phone. She has much more free time and needs much less quiet time than her friend. The women have promised to talk by phone once a month and get together in person at least once a month, a schedule that Lee is quite happy with. Carson, on the other hand, would like some kind of weekly contact, even if it is just a 20 minute phone call. In order to preserve the relationship, both people acknowledge that they need to come to some resolution and reveal their own feelings or emotions, to themselves as well as to the other.

Using the Skills Intra-psychically. Lee suggested that she and Carson meet to talk about the problem but first take some time to reflect personally about what might be going on that was affecting the situation. Upon first reflection, Lee found she was a little angry and frustrated that Carson was pressing her for more time. She began to question why she was so upset when Carson just wanted to spend more time with her. It was not like she was asking her to do something work related. She wrote down her thinking and condensed it to two major thoughts. First, she found herself complaining that Carson should know that her work schedule was demanding and she needed more quiet time. She also found herself surprisingly resentful that Carson had so much more free time than she did. Lee could see that these were unrealistic expectations of her friend and that her jealousy might be affecting her willingness to get together more often. She decided to take these two thoughts and reframe them into something more positive and solution focused. Her first reframe was, "It is not Carson's job to understand how stressed out and overworked I am. It is unfair to be angry when I am really upset with myself for not having a better handle on my work life." She followed this by writing, "I am actually glad Carson has a job with lots of free time because she is more flexible and can meet my busier schedule. I love Carson and know she is enjoying her slower pace after raising three kids on her own." After she wrote down these more positive reframes, Lee found that her anger had dissipated and she was feeling more optimistic about resolving this with Carson.

Carson knew that her feelings about this issue were hurt and guilt. She was hurt that Lee would not spend more time with her and guilty because she also knew Lee was overworked. She wrote her thinking down as, "I feel hurt and rejected. Lee just doesn't want to spend time with me anymore. Maybe the friendship is just over." Her second series of statement were focused on her anger. "Lee only thinks about her own needs and I keep bending over backwards to make my schedule fit hers. Then, when we do finally find a time that works for her, she cancels half the time because she is sick or tired. I am really angry about this!" Lee was surprised at how upset she was about this and did not want to take this kind of resentment into their first meeting. She spent some time reframing these statements into positive options. Her first reframe was about the hurt and rejection, "I feel a little too hurt about this for it not to be about something else. I think it reminds me of times when school friends rejected me in high school when I was going through a rough time. But, Lee always stuck by me through thick and thin. Our friendship is not over it is just going through a rough patch." Carson also looked at how angry she was with Lee and realized she was being unfair so she restated her comments, "Lee is my very best and oldest friend and I can see how she is running herself ragged. Instead of being resentful, I should be concerned for her and also grateful that my own life is more manageable. There were times in my past when I was so busy that I am sure I neglected her as well." These reframes allowed Carson to remember times when they were very close as well as a time when she was not available. She found her emotions moved up to compassion and hoped that they would indeed work this out.

Using the Skills Interpersonally. Lee and Carson met and decided to each share what they had discovered in listening to and reframing their own self-talk. They decided to take turns asking each other questions about the dilemma. Lee started by asking, "Carson, what about this issue is most difficult for you." Carson replied, "I want to spend enough time with you that I still feel we are an integral part of one another's lives. But, when something comes up and I want to call you, I am afraid that I will just be a bother and you will see me as a pest." Lee reflected Carson's words verbatim and then Carson asked her a question, "I just want to know if you still want to be friends or if your busy life is too full for the kind of friendship we used to have." Lee responded, "Carson, you are my best friend and I cannot imagine not having you in my life. I am starting to realize that my life is out of control. It feels like my life is on fire. If I don't do something soon, I will be dead or have no friends or family left."

Carson reflected back Lee's statement and then tried to reframe it for her. "Lee, I hear you saying that you do want me as your best friend. It also sounds like your life is pretty overwhelming and that worries you because you might lose a friendship like ours." This reframe excluded the comments about work "killing her" and being "out of control" so Lee could take a breath and not be overly dramatic about her work life. This allowed her to see it as a problem to be addressed instead of a raging fire that would burn her up. It also helped Carson see that this was not personal; Lee was having trouble with many relationships because of her schedule. Carson commented, "Lee, is there something I can do to help you? I know this meeting is about spending more time together but mostly it's about our friendship. I want to be here for you and not be just one more thing that stresses you out." Lee paused and then she reflected and responded to her comment. "Carson it sounds like you want to help me and be my friend. You also don't want to be just one more thing that stresses me out. That is what is so crazy about my life. I can't seem to take time to nurture myself because I am so tired. It's like I forget how much I need time with you and my family."

Carson took a moment and reminded Lee about the time her own life was out of control. "I lost perspective back then, Lee. Remember how stressed out I was? And, you would check in on me and take me out to dinner so I did not have to cook after a hard day at work. Maybe that is what you need from me? Do you want me to be more assertive in getting together?" Lee laughed and said, "Yes, I guess that is what I need from you. I think I just get so used to helping other people all week that I forget that I need help. It seems ridiculous that I need help just remembering to have fun. I feel like a fraud when I can't even manage my own life." Carson reflected back and reframed, "Lee, I hear you say that you need help from me in the same way you once helped me. It sounds like all the focus you have helping other people all week makes you forget to focus on yourself. You need help remembering to have fun and perhaps believe as a therapist you should not have to."

The two friends continued their exploration of what was preventing them from getting together and how this affected each of them. As they deepened their understanding of what they needed, unencumbered by disempowering emotions and expectations, they began to see a path forward. Carson realized that she needed to reach out to other people and get out more. Her business was leaving her increasingly isolated and she asked Lee if she had ideas of how she might do that. Lee was more than happy to offer suggestions that she often made with clients who were feeling alone. Lee was more relaxed after the conversation and able to look calmly at a situation that seemed so out of control before they started talking. She and Carson brainstormed options about having a more balanced life, and in doing so, found more consistency in their own relationship. In this case, the *Touchstone Skills* allowed them to solve their joint issue through patient questioning, reflecting, and reframing the content in a way that would help them come to shared solutions.

Using the Touchstone Skills in the Workplace

The first example of using the *Touchstone Skills* in the workplace takes place between two co-workers, Marco and Richard, who work together in the customer service division of a large internet marketing company. Marco is American born and of Puerto Rican descent. Richard, who is 15 years older than Marco, immigrated to the states from England 20 years ago. Marco has been frustrated working with Richard because their conversations seem to consistently result in misunderstandings. In terms of their communication styles, Marco is much more of an extrovert and says what he thinks most of the time. Richard, on the other hand, processes situations internally for some time before he makes a comment and is often left feeling pressured and misunderstood in his meetings with Marco.

Marco and Richard have been assigned to a project with a two-month deadline and, in their first meeting; they agreed to use the *Touchstone Skills* as a path to improve their communication skills. At their first meeting, they both shared the emotions that were most prevalent about the dilemma. Each man reported that he felt discouraged because of the intensity of the disempowering emotions, which were expressed as relatively high levels of guilt and anger about working together. However, they also recognized that these were emotions that could be channeled into productive change as opposed to more debilitating emotions such as despair. They also noted that they each had some empowering emotions which manifested as low intensity feelings of happiness, pride and, hopefulness.

The men agreed that it was encouraging to see that neither man was having overly intense disempowering feelings that might make this process much more difficult. Yet they were also surprised to acknowledge that they were equally discouraged and not experiencing positive emotions with any great intensity. Richard remarked that he was most concerned about not experiencing high levels of happiness or pride. Marco concurred but added, "At least neither of us is blaming the other and we both shared feelings of hopefulness. But, I would like to have a sense of pride moving forward and certainly more understanding of where we are both coming from." Richard agreed and suggested they each take time to go through the intra-psychic application of the *Touchstone Skills* and then meet again in a week.

Marco's intra-psychic questioning and reflecting. Marco went home and committed to use the skills of intra-psychic communication. He decided to use a tape recorder and set up the process as if he was a reporter interviewing himself. He began by asking himself, "What concerns me about working with Richard?" Marco answered, "I feel like we are oil and water and just cannot communicate well. I think he is pretty weird and I can't stand his continually mumbling 'Hmmmm' every time I speak." He reflected back, "So, I feel like oil and water when I talk to Richard and I think he is weird. And, I cannot stand his mannerism of saying 'Hmmm' in response to my speaking." Marco reflected back to himself, "Yes, he acts so superior and judgmental." He reflected back again, "So, I think he is acting superior and judgmental. Does he remind me of anyone from my past?" Marco thought a moment and answered, "Yes, as a matter of fact he reminds me of my last boss. He never gave me feedback but just sat there like a rock. Then, out of the blue one day he fired me and had nothing to say about why."

Marco's reframing. Marco continued the process of taping the conversation with himself for about twenty minutes and then listened back to his words so he could begin to reframe the content into a more positive joint solution. He started with the first two statements, "So, it sounds like I think that Richard and I are very different and have trouble communicating. I find some of his mannerisms difficult to overcome. I find his use of 'hmmm' particularly challenging. It also sounds like I believe he might be judging me, perhaps even seeing me as inferior." Marco noted that when he removed the derogatory words like "weird", "superior", and "cannot stand" he began to relax and not feel so angry. The replacement words such as "very different", "trouble communicating", and "particularly challenging" all moved him from an accusatory stance to one of contemplation. He then reframed the statement about his boss, "It sounds like Richard reminds me of my old boss at my last job. He was a quiet guy like Richard and would not give me any feedback. It felt really unfair because he fired me without giving me the opportunity to change whatever it was that was bothering him. But, Richard is not my boss. He is a co-worker and he probably wants respect and harmony in the workplace as much as I do." This statement reflects both reframing and perspective shifting by Marco.

Richard's intra-psychic questioning and reflecting. Richard reviewed the *Touchstone Skills* as a way to begin his self-talk. He was a writer in his spare time so he decided to add the questioning and reflecting processes to his journal each day before the meeting. Each day, he asked one question, reflected it back, and then reframed it into a more positive joint solution. His first question was one he asked whenever he had an inordinate amount of trepidation with another person, "Richard, is there something about this situation or person that is bringing up the past?" He wrote for some time about a similar situation he had when he first arrived in the United States to attend a prestigious university. He was very shy and homesick and did not understand the informality of Americans when they spoke. Much more verbal at home, he found himself grow more introverted and quiet for fear of being made a fool of. Richard summarized this writing by noting, "It sounds like this trouble communicating with Marco reminds me of the struggles I had at college. I believe that experience made me more introverted and quiet than I really am." He then asked, "So, what about Marco in particular is bringing this up?" "Well', he wrote, "Marco is like an American after ten pots of coffee. He just talks and talks and has a sense of humor that is so quick and biting, I want to scream at him to shut up. I end up just nodding my head half the time because I cannot keep up processing all the information coming my way. I can tell it makes him angry and I know he probably thinks I am "slow". The stress is driving me crazy."

Richard's intra-psychic reframing. Richard began shifting his perspective, in the spirit of a reframe, to say, "It sounds like college was really a hard time for me. I was shy and homesick and had a lot of trouble with the American's less formal communication styles. Although that was years ago, this situation with Marco brings up those old negative feelings again." Richard was careful to remove any statements from his writing that were self-deprecating. He also highlighted the fact that the feelings may be familiar but the situation, time of life, and person in question were all very different. He was able to see that although the past could not be changed, this might be an opportunity to interact in a different, more authentic manner. He shifted his perspective about Marco with a softer interpretation: "Marco speaks very fast and I have trouble keeping up. Instead of saying something directly to him, I just nod my head. Inside I am very angry and frustrated, but outside I just get quieter and quieter. I can see this dynamic does not work for him either because he looks on the outside like I feel on the inside." By removing all the negative adverbs and adjectives, Richard is able to restate the issues as a shared problem that is difficult for both of them. His reframe of the situation begins to mirror Marco's, in the form of a joint solution: "We both want respect and harmony in the workplace." This is a reframe that produces hope for change and resolution.

Interpersonal questioning. Richard and Marco met a week later to begin their interpersonal communication process. They flipped a coin to see who would begin the questioning process and Richard went first. He asked Marco what had him discouraged about working together. Marco responded, "Richard, you seem like a nice guy but half the time I never know what you are thinking or how you arrived at a conclusion. I need to talk through things and understand how we came to the ideas in the project. I cannot imagine how two such different people can work together effectively." Marco then asked

Richard what his concerns were. Richard smiled and said, "Marco, I have just the opposite issue. Sometimes, when you start talking about a project, I cannot keep up with all the ideas and where you are heading. It drives me crazy inside." Richard asked a deeper question, "So, it sounds as if the trouble is not that you don't like me, it is that you don't like the way I process information and come to a conclusion without you. Is that true?" Marco responded, "Oh, yeah, it is not personal in terms of you being a bad guy. I am just afraid we will fail as a team and I will lose my job." Marco asked Richard, "Help me understand what you need to be successful?" Richard spent some time talking about his need for collaboration, pacing, and time to think without interruption, in order to feel respected and gain harmony in the workplace.

Interpersonal reflecting. Next, the two men decided to use reflecting to work on building their *Touchstone Skills* to result in a better communication strategy between them. Marco started by reflecting Richard's first statement, "It sounds like you have trouble keeping up with me and I start talking about my ideas and concerns and it drives you crazy inside." Richard nods affirmatively and then reflects back Marco's earlier statement, "Marco, it sounds like you think I am a nice guy but you cannot figure out what I am thinking or how I came to certain conclusions. You need to talk through things and understand how conclusions were arrived at. You cannot imagine how we can work together given these differences." Next, Richard reflected, "Marco, it sounds like your concerns are not about me being a bad guy but that you feel that, as team, we will fail. You are worried about losing your job if that happens." Marco then summarizes Richard's response about what he needs to be successful, "Richard, I hear you saying that you need time to think through a project without interruptions. You also need me to stop talking so fast and interrupting you with my ideas and my jokes. You also need to have a collaborative process but feel it would take too much time for us to be effective."

The men decided to continue reflecting for a bit before moving on to reframing. Marco began by stating, "Your comment about my talking fast reminds me of other feedback I have received over the years from my wife and friends. People tend to joke that I need slow down and smell the roses. They also tell me I am exciting and passionate and a great thinker." Richard reflected back, "So, it sounds like you really thought about this comment and it made you think about some feedback that others have given you that you are both someone who moves fast and may miss things and yet you are also a passionate and exciting thinker." "Yes," Marco remarked, "it makes me think that you might help slow me down and balance me out." Richard reflected, "So, you see that this arrangement might actually slow you down and balance out your thinking." Marco nodded in agreement.

Richard followed by sharing, "Marco, it took me a long time to know that my need to go slow was not a sign of weakness but just how I process information. I really need time to take an idea deep inside and then I start connecting it to other ideas. It is like I start building this web inside my head where all the things just said connect and form a bigger idea." Marco reflected "So, it seems you understand that you need to take time to integrate new information and that it actually brings more creativity to your process." Richard shook his head in agreement and added, "It is also a painful process because I can see that people get frustrated with me. And, when I sense the frustration, I become withdrawn and my creative process gets derailed because I am shutting down inside and outside." Marco reflected, "So, it sounds like this creative process can get derailed when you sense other people are frustrated and you withdraw in response." The conversation continued in this manner throughout the lunch and Marco and Richard began to feel more connected with one another as they sensed a common understanding of one another's strengths and challenges. This led to a renewed sense of respect for each other, resulting in greater harmony in the workplace.

Interpersonal reframing. Several days later, the men met for a final time before the project started the following week. They decided to take the information that they had learned from one another and create positive reframes in the form of joint solutions, separate from and transcending any fear of failure or judgment of themselves or one another. They agreed to each consider the other's perspectives, to reframe the other's statements about their processing and fear of working together into a problem solving framework. Richard restated his issue with working together and fear of failing, demonstrating a shift in his own perspective. "I need time to think about ideas and then make connections and come up with my own ideas and solutions. I don't see how that can happen with you being so fast and such an extrovert. I am afraid the project will be a complete disaster and we will end up hating each other." Marco then provided a possible solution. "It sounds like if we work together, you need time to think about the ideas I come up with so you can be more creative. You are afraid of failing because I work so fast and, being an extrovert, I process out loud. Yet, we might be a powerful team. I hear that you want to find a solution to this." Marco then restated his concerns and Richard reframed them as, "Marco, it sounds like you are worried that you will be frustrated with the time I need to process information and worry the anger might build and ruin the project. If also sounds like you need the freedom to brainstorm and talk without feeling constrained by my need for time. It also sounds like you see that we could be a powerful team because we have these differences. So, how do we create a process that allows each of us to hold respect and maintain harmony in the workplace?"

In this case, the two co-workers decided to spend the first day on the project finding a way that honored their differences. It was not always easy, but they found a way to create enough structure and silence for Richard while leaving ample time for Marco to outwardly process his ideas. Richard found that as long as he did not have to view each of Marco's ideas as an action item, he was able to relax and listen to his creative bursts of energy. By using reflecting and reframing, he was also able to slow the conversation down in order to give them both time to be sure they understood one another. Marco found that instead of peppering Richard with questions when he was quiet, he would just check in and see if he needed some time before they moved on. Richard was surprised to hear that his use of "hmmm" was so irritating because he meant it to cover up his inner frustration. Now, he could just drop the façade and offer a more authentic response. Their commitment to this pathway and to respecting one another resulted in a more integrated and harmonious workplace than either could have produced alone or with someone who had a similar way of processing information. At the end of the project, Richard decided to review their feelings. He was amazed to find that he had intensified his empowering emotions and even noticed more subtle shifts toward less intensity of disempowering emotions. Additionally, he noted that his other relationships at work were much more cordial as he applied the skills of questioning, reflecting, and reframing to everyday conversations.

Now that you have seen the *Touchstone Skills* applied to family, friends, and workplace colleagues, we will advance to the actual footsteps, beginning with revealing emotions and empowerment. The next chapter will present these two processes and provide you with surveys to measure your levels of emotional competence and empowerment. The chapter will conclude with a case scenario that applies the use of the *Touchstone Skills* to these to processes along the pathway.

Chapter Three
Revealing Emotions and Empowerment

Overview

Now that you have been introduced the *Touchstone Skills* and explored how these are applied to specific case scenarios, we will turn your attention to the six footsteps along the pathway. It is our contention that the success of our interpersonal relationships is directly proportional to the journey found through the process of following the six footsteps, which are supported by the three *Touchstone Skills* we employ in self-talk and dialogue. In this chapter, we will illustrate the first two steps on the pathway, that of revealing our emotions and empowerment. We begin with an examination of these concepts and how they relate to resolving everyday dilemmas, followed by a survey to help you determine your competency and to encourage you to develop a deeper capacity to embody these ideals. We will focus on the development of mindfulness as a means to enhance greater self-awareness and deepen your practice of these two important *footstep processes*. The chapter concludes with a case study that will demonstrate the *Touchstone Skills* and how they relate to these two footsteps.

The Importance of Identifying Emotions

In the book, *In Justice, InAccord* (2012), the authors developed the thesis, supported by others in the field of psychology, that initially identifying emotions is critical to the conflict resolution process. Until disputants identify their emotions (overt or underlying) they cannot make effective use of the principles of authenticity or the practice of the *Touchstone Skills*. These same principles of authenticity and the practice of the *Touchstone Skills* apply to the role of emotions in everyday life, where people confront problem-solving and decision making situations. These emotions can serve to facilitate progress in communication or they can hinder it. Thus, it is important for you to learn to identify your emotions at the outset in preparation for any dialogue with another.

For many years in the professional literature, emotions, primarily negative effects, were given short shrift. They were viewed as destructive, divisive, and debilitating. Then, beginning in the 1990's, a powerful new wave of thought ushered in what was called a "functional role of emotions," and this was heralded as the "new look" (Campos, Munne, Kermoian, & Campos, 1994; Saarni, Campos, Camrus, & Witherton, 2006). These theorists resurrected some of the thinking of brilliant historical scholars, such as Charles Darwin and William James, upon whose observations they amplified many important evolutionary functions of negative emotions (Ries & Harter, 2012; Harter, 2012). Four general functions have now been identified.

1. Emotions have a protective value, as both Darwin (1872, 1965) and James (1890) cogently argued, since they prepare one for fight or flight.
2. Emotions provide organizational and motivational functions. For instance, an appropriate, intermediate level of anxiety or anger might actually help individuals organize their behavior toward a particular goal.
3. Emotions also act as signals to others in interpersonal communication. For example, sadness or depression may elicit an empathic reaction in significant others.
4. Emotions, conscious or unconscious, are also signals to the *self*, in that they can provide insights into one's motives. They can provide clues as to what is important in one's life. They can also facilitate particular future actions that may help to repair some of the minor hurt in everyday relationships. Emotions not expressed or not labeled can be become maladaptive in a relationship.

In Justice, InAccord (2012) broadened this thinking of the importance of negative emotions to include the powerful role of positive emotions, as well. Other contemporary psychologists concur. For example, Frederickson (1998) has decried the fact that the focus has been entirely on negative emotions, such as anger, guilt, or anxiety, as if positive emotions, such as happiness, optimism, or hopefulness, have little functional value and are viewed as relatively superfluous, irrelevant to survival. In this section of the chapter, we will focus on the broader range of both positive and negative emotions, including the importance of developing more expertise in identifying and understanding emotional responses of self and other, as they relate directly to the *Touchstone Skills*. We will also touch on the notion that negative and positive emotions can exist simultaneously and demonstrate this concept using both Western research (Harter, 1999) and eastern Buddhist philosophies, such as Hahn (2013), that stress the importance of acknowledging that one must appreciate the mutual and reciprocal nature of seeming contradictory feelings.

Before You Communicate with Another, Know Your Emotions

It is critical for people to identify their own emotions as accurately as possible before attempting to engage in dialogue, especially those that focus on problem solving or other difficulties. Toward this goal, the first author, Ries, on the basis or her own clinical, mediation, and arbitration practice, identified several emotions that she has demonstrated are important in the reception and use of the *Touchstone Skills*. In her earlier book *In Justice, InAccord* (Ries & Harter, 2012) she grouped these emotions into two categories, empowering (positive) emotions and disempowering (negative) emotions, anticipating that an acceptance and mastery of the *Touchstone Skills* would enhance the empowering emotions and attenuate or weaken the strength of the disempowering emotions. And this is precisely what the authors found; that empowering emotions, such as happiness, contentment, and empathy, increased in intensity when using the *Touchstone Skills* and disempowering emotions, such as depression, humiliation, and despair, decreased as a result of using the *Touchstone Skills*.

Although this conceptualization is decidedly Western, it is compatible with Eastern Buddhist perspectives on different classifications of emotions. For example, the Dalai Lama (2011) distinguishes between those emotions that are beneficial and those that are harmful, to the point of being interpersonally destructive. This, he points out, is particularly problematic where their intensity is disproportionate to the situation in which they arise. Destructive emotions can erode our capacity for genuine contentment and undermine our mental equilibrium, both of which are necessary for authentic communication.

But let us return to the specific emotions in each of our two groups (Ries & Harter, 2012). The complete list of empowering or positive emotions includes pride, gratefulness, happiness, contentment, empathy, and hopefulness. The complete list of disempowering or negative emotions includes anger, guilt, anxiety, depression, humiliation, and despair. Those in the bottom half of the disempowering emotions are the most debilitating. To the extent that learning the value of authenticity coupled with an attempt to master the *Touchstone Skills* is successful, then these most negative emotions should lessen in intensity, as the individual feels more empowered to engage in effective communication strategies.

It should be noted that a number of the emotions depart from the conventional lists of affects such as happiness, pride, anger, and depression. These more commonly identified emotions are included. However, we have also added terms that we consider "emotion—cognitive hybrids", such as hopeful, contented, despair (see Ries & Harter, 2012, for a complete discussion of these issues, including a justification for so doing). In these combinations or hybrids, it is difficult to tease apart the separate role of an emotion versus a cognition, because they are powerful combinations, in consort. Interestingly, in the classic Buddhist theory of mind, there is no concept of "emotion" as a single category, nor is there a word that exactly translates into the English word of "emotion." Rather, all mental states are understood to include both cognitive and "feeling" dimensions (Dalai Lama, 2011).

Some of the implications of the emotions in our own lists may surprise the reader. Noteworthy is the emotion of anger. While anger can be debilitating, if it is at a reasonable and manageable level, it can be harnessed toward progress in communication. If monitored appropriately, it can serve as a signal that one cares enough about an issue or a person to be angry, and can then mobilize one toward effective action. Ries (Ries & Harter, 2012) has argued that anger can be important to understand as a central emotional force necessary to move people toward the resolution of a problem-solving situation.

Here again we see consistencies between our view of anger and Eastern Buddhist perspectives. As the Dalai Lama (2011) points out, in some situations, anger may combine with strong compassion, or may accompany a sense of injustice. Feeling angry, if expressed moderately, can, in the short run, make your mind more focused and may provide an extra burst of energy and determination. This energy, in turn, may help you become more effective in obtaining the goals you rightfully seek. Anger, from our perspective, can be productive, in the context of learning the *Touchstone Skills*, particularly if it leads to movement toward more positive, empowering emotions. It can serve as a signal that one needs to implement the skills of questioning, reflecting, and reframing.

In a subsequent section in this chapter, we will introduce you to a brief emotions survey, which you will fill out yourself. This will offer you a profile of where you stand in terms of the empowering (positive) and disempowering (negative) emotions that you may bring to an interpersonal decision-making or problem-solving situation in everyday life. We will include the survey, after a brief excursion in an important goal within the field of emotions, namely, the normative elements of emotional competence and set the stage for an appreciation of the balance between negative and positive emotions, how they should not be conceptualized as a competing duality. We will explore, based on research findings, the challenge of combining negative with positive emotions in our affective experiences, toward more authentic communication.

Socio-Emotional Competence

The goals of this volume are very much in synchrony with developmental models of what has been termed "emotional competence" (Saarni et al., 2006), which underscores the importance of a sequence of stages through which people progress in order to effectively appreciate and understand their own emotional reactions. A complete discussion of this eight-stage sequence and their links to the *InAccord Conflict Analysis*® model can be found in Ries & Harter, (2012). However, key concepts involve an awareness of one's emotions, not as easy a task as this might imply, since some feelings tend to become masked beyond recognition. We find that our Emotion Survey, soon to be described, helps people to become more aware of their complex feelings.

Emotional competence also involves the realization that one's inner emotional states may not directly correspond to the emotions that we may overtly express toward others who are important to us. For example, a hidden emotion of feeling "hurt" may be masked by an outward expression of anger that needs to be harnessed and clarified. Thus, self-regulatory strategies need to be invoked, to weaken the intensity of disruptive emotions and to strengthen the intensity of the empowering emotions that can lead to more effective problem-solving strategies. Emotional understanding also involves an appreciation for what the other person is feeling. The *Touchstone Skills* and the *footstep processes* will aid in the forming of such perspective taking. Our point is that aversive emotions must be labeled and dealt with before effective problem solutions can be entertained. Moreover, they must be viewed in consort with positive emotions, where a goal is movement toward a greater balance of positive emotions. We address these issues, before presenting the survey for you to complete.

Harmonizing negative and positive feelings. From a cognitive-developmental perspective, the mind of the young child is naturally fractionated, that is concepts are sorted into clear dichotomies, for example, good versus bad; nice versus mean; smart versus dumb; and boy versus girl, which dictates rigid gender-stereotypic roles, behaviors, toys, and dress. These distinctions, manifested as black-and-white thinking, extend to young children's emotional understanding (Harter, 1999). One must be "all mad" or "all happy"; the two cannot be simultaneously experienced. With increasing cognitive development (Fischer, 1980; Harter, 1999) this all-or-none thinking gradually abates as older children come to realize that one can be nice and mean, smart and dumb, happy and sad.

However, there is a somewhat paradoxical recapitulation during adolescence, adeptly explained by a leading cognitive-developmentalist, Kurt Fischer (1980). Fischer points out that whenever there is movement to a new level of cognitive development, for example, with the emergence of the ability to think more abstractly in adolescence, one has difficulty in "cognitive controlling" these new acquisitions. Think about an analogy when one is learning a new sport, such as tennis. There is a lack of physical control of new movements, one hits the ball out of the court or into the net or makes shots that are readily returnable by an opponent. The mind, encountering the need to master new abstract cognitive skills makes similar errors, one of which is a seeming return to all-or-none thinking, albeit at a more abstract level. So now one is intelligent at one point in time, totally mentally incompetent at another point in time. The adolescent feels ecstatic in one situation and then switches to the depths of despair in another situation making these inexplicable switches in self-perceptions or emotional states extremely distressing for them (Harter, 1999).

The ability to pair a positive emotion with a negative emotion and be comfortable with the contrast is an inordinately difficult task whether you are an adolescent or adult. However, this task can be made easier by the support of a strong social system of people who can help normalize this clash of contradictory emotional responses. Fischer and colleagues (Fischer, 1980; Fischer & Biddell, 2006) provide very compelling findings as they cogently argue that the higher one ascends toward more mature stages of cognitive development, particularly during the later stages of abstract thinking, the more one needs the support or "scaffolding" from mature socializing agents. These could include various mentors, such as family members, older siblings, teachers, coaches, support groups, pastors, counselors, therapists, or mediators. There could be numerous sources of people to nurture and support higher levels of understanding of what seemed to be dichotomies. For those of us fortunate enough to have had one or two of these wise mentors, we can remember and integrate their advice and support into an internal support system.

This discussion of paired emotional experiences converges with Western conceptualizations of all-or-none emotional thought and Buddhist Eastern perspectives on the dualistic thinking that many adults apply to their own affective experience. Thich Nhat Hanh (2013) describes just such a scenario, suggesting that feelings become isolated from one another. This occurs when painful emotions are buried, denied, or misunderstood and positive emotions exaggerated, or the reverse can be true. For Hanh, a solution to the discomfort of contrasting emotions can be found in a sense of community, relying on the Buddhist concept of the "Sangha," a supportive group that guides, protects, and supports it members. The reliance on more mature individuals, who have struggled with their own emotions, bringing wisdom to their own experiences, can be beneficial to those caught up in the dualism of positive versus negative emotions. Harter's (1999, 2012) interpretation is that the ability to cut through the dualism of positive versus negative emotions can be aided by further cognitive development, normalization of mixed emotions, and the support of caring and thoughtful adults who bring their own wisdom to the experience.

Balancing Positive and Negative Emotions

A key concept in our footstep pathway is the balance between positive and negative emotions, once they can be simultaneously experienced. Consider a situation in which one feels both happy and sad toward an individual or both excited but angry. Harter and colleagues (Harter, 1999) have revealed that the balance or the intensity of the two emotions can dramatically impact the degree of conflict that is provoked. Their studies reveal that if the strength of the *negative* emotion in the pair, such as sadness or anger, far outweighs the experience of the *positive* emotion, then more conflict in the situation will be experienced. If the balance was in favor of the positive emotion, far less conflict was reported. Participants in these studies were also asked to rate the degree to which they perceived these two emotions to be opposites. The results demonstrated that the greater the participant's perception of opposites, the more they reported conflict in the interpersonal situation.

Why, one might ask, could such seemingly polarized emotions *not* be considered opposites? Our participants explained why. For example, those who did not see happiness or anger as total opposites cited reasons such as, "They are similar because they both energize you". or "They can both mobilize you to take some productive action." Those who saw "happy and sad" as more similar commented that "It's like an experience that is bittersweet, you are sad that your friends are moving on but happy that they might have a better life." This echoes a sentiment set forth by poet Kahil Gibran (1923) who spoke of the harmony of joy and sorrow when he wrote, "Your joy is your sorrow unmasked. And the selfsame well from which your laughter rises was oftentimes filled with your tears" (p.29).

Survey on the Intensity of Your Own Emotions

The first step in this survey is to think about a significant situation in your interpersonal life with someone you care about that is not a major conflict or acute dispute. We recommend you find an interpersonal situation where you and others need to come to an agreement about a course of action. The reasoning for choosing a less significant dispute is that, for now, we want to keep it manageable in order to learn the use of the footsteps. We suggest that the discussion of the *Touchstone Skills* will be more effective, if the people involved can first identify and share their emotions. Your survey responses may open up a discussion with those involved in the dilemma that may widen the horizon of your interpretation of the situation.

The first six emotions are empowering, the second group of six emotions are more disempowering (although *anger* may be on the

73

cusp.). If you wish, you could compute an average for both. All of these particular emotions are scored 4, 3, 2, 1. High scores for the two groups reflect high levels of feeling either or both of these emotions. Low scores mean that these emotions are not that intense. Your score may be different for the two groups of emotions; however, this will give you some indication of the balance of the two groups of emotions. So attend to the relative strengths of these two sets of emotions, the positive versus the negative emotions. For example, you might be higher on the positive empowering emotions, but lower on the disempowering, or negative, emotions. Alternatively, you may be lower on the positive empowering emotions and higher on the disempowering emotions.

My Feelings Survey

Check the box next to the emotion that best describes the intensity or strength of each feeling **with regard to a particular situation that requires either decision making or problem solving, or both**. Sum up your scores for the first six emotions and divide by six. The higher your score, the more intensely you experience the empowering emotions. Sum up your scores from items seven through twelve and divide by six; the higher your score the more intense your disempowering emotions.

1) Pride

☐ Very Strong (4) ☐ Pretty Strong (3) ☐ Not that strong (2) ☐ Not strong at all (1)

2) Gratefulness

☐ Very Strong (4) ☐ Pretty Strong (3) ☐ Not that strong (2) ☐ Not strong at all (1)

3) Happiness

☐ Very Strong (4) ☐ Pretty Strong (3) ☐ Not that strong (2) ☐ Not strong at all (1)

4) Contentment

☐ Very Strong (4) ☐ Pretty Strong (3) ☐ Not that strong (2) ☐ Not strong at all (1)

5) Empathy

☐ Very Strong (4) ☐ Pretty Strong (3) ☐ Not that strong (2) ☐ Not strong at all (1)

6) Hopefulness

☐ Very Strong (4) ☐ Pretty Strong (3) ☐ Not that strong (2) ☐ Not strong at all (1)

7) Anger

☐ Very Strong (4) ☐ Pretty Strong (3) ☐ Not that strong (2) ☐ Not strong at all (1)

8) Guilt

☐ Very Strong (4) ☐ Pretty Strong (3) ☐ Not that strong (2) ☐ Not strong at all (1)

9) Anxiety

☐ Very Strong (4) ☐ Pretty Strong (3) ☐ Not that strong (2) ☐ Not strong at all (1)

10) Depression

☐ Very Strong (4) ☐ Pretty Strong (3) ☐ Not that strong (2) ☐ Not strong at all (1)

11) Humiliation

☐ Very Strong (4) ☐ Pretty Strong (3) ☐ Not that strong (2) ☐ Not strong at all (1)

12) Despair

☐ Very Strong (4) ☐ Pretty Strong (3) ☐ Not that strong (2) ☐ Not strong at all (1)

It may be instructive for you to revisit this survey, after you have had opportunities to put the practice of the *Touchstone Skills* in place in your own life, in order to assess if there has been a change in your emotional reactions. This should provide a backdrop to how you might respond to the materials presented in the next section. These are designed to move people toward the more positive emotions without denying the negative emotions, but rather defusing their intensity. This in turn should facilitate greater communication toward decision-making solutions.

Emotions Revealed through Mindfulness

In this section, we introduce the concept of mindfulness, noting that your committed practice to the *Touchstone Skills* and the *footstep processes* actually enhances mindfulness through quiet self-reflection and careful attention to your dialogue with others. Mindfulness, a state of being in the here and now, serves as a way to be in touch with your emotions. It creates a "state of consciousness" which involves attending to your moment-to-moment experience (Brown & Ryan, 2003). This is important to understand if we are dedicated to acting and communicating our feelings from a more self-aware and, therefore, more self-liberating mindset. Mediation is the most common practice associated with mindfulness. In this section, we use a mindfulness framework developed by Shapiro, S. L., Carlson, L. E., Astin, J. A. and Freedman, B. (2006) as potential structure for your commitment to the practice of the *Touchstone Skills* and the *footstep processes*.

Shapiro, et al. (2006) present their framework for mindfulness by breaking it down into three constructs: 1) *Intention,* which is some kind of personal vision that can be both dynamic and evolving; 2) *Attention,* which is suspending all ways of interpreting experience and attending to experience itself; and 3) *Attitude,* which is what we bring to the act of paying attention. Our theory contends that these three components can be enhanced by the use of the *Touchstone Skills* and *the footstep processes* with oneself and others. Alternatively, the three components serve to deepen your practice of the *Skills* and *processes* enhancing your ability to move toward greater self-liberation. Although we will break these three components into separate discussions in the following pages, they are not separate but "interwoven aspects of a single cyclic process and occur simultaneously" (Shapiro et al., 2006, p. 375) in the same way that the *Touchstone Skills* and *footstep processes* weave together a cyclical journey that happens concurrently.

Intention. Your intention is your vision of why you are engaging in a mindfulness practice in the first place. The *Touchstone Skills* and *footstep processes* are the practice tools that begin your journey along the pathway, as you set your intention to not merely practice these skills, but embody them as you move toward self-liberation. The importance of establishing your intention was highlighted in a study by D.H. Shapiro (1992) that explored the intentions of meditation practitioners and found that as they continued to practice their intentions, they began to shift from self-exploration to self-regulation and eventually to self-liberation. This study also found that outcomes correlated with intentions, meaning that what you intend at the beginning of your journey had a high probability of becoming your reality as you progress. Longtime meditator, trainer, and researcher Jon Kabat-Zinn (1990) emphasized the importance of intention when he revealed that he once believed that the mindfulness practice of meditation was so powerful in and of itself that all he had to do was practice it and he would see growth and change. However, with time he came to see that some kind of personal intention was necessary for self-liberation to occur. We counsel that if you set your intentions to practice the skills along the pathway, you will have a more meaningful and rewarding practice, and if you set your intentions to use these skills as part of a larger journey to self-liberation, you will also have a more meaningful and rewarding life.

Using the Touchstone Skills to Decrease the Intensity of Negative Emotions

The ability to be aware of and comfortable with your negative emotions allows you to more easily tolerate them and liberate from them. Our theory follows that through the practice of the *Touchstone Skills* and *footstep processes* you can gradually expand your ability to tolerate emotional dissonance by the constant exposure of questioning, reflecting and reframing. These techniques guide you out of reactionary or habitual engagement and into greater objectivity, thus, making your subjective experience objective. Shapiro et al. (2006) notes that your capacity to witness your current situation can help you tolerate very strong negative emotions with greater objectivity and less reactivity. This ability expands over time with repeated exposure to the point where one learns that emotions, thoughts, and body sensations are not as frightening as once experienced (Segal, Williams, & Teasdale, 2002). This process of objectively witnessing your emotions and building up a tolerance for ones that are unpleasant, leads to the second construct of mindfulness, which Shapiro refers to as attention.

Attention. The *Touchstone Skills* of questioning, reflecting, and reframing each serve the practice of mindful attention to your experience, which supports healthy communication. Practice of these skills and processes allows you to re-enter the experience with greater emotional clarity, more complete knowledge of the thoughts that may be influencing the moment and a broader perspective of the views and experiences that every person brings to bear on solving a dilemma or problem. Attention is a critical element of our pathway and, indeed, the state of consciousness that is called mindfulness, as you learn to pay attention to the *footstep processes* of revealing emotions, empowerment, gaining perspective, empathy and compassion, authenticity, and transparency. Attention is also a tenet of many mental health therapies such as Gestalt therapy, wherein founder Fritz Perls (1966) defined two powerful cognitive abilities that enable you to be in the present moment, vigilance, which is the capacity to attend for long periods of time on a single experience, and switching, which is the willful capability to shift your focus of attention from one emotional state to another. The intra-psychic application of the *Touchstone Skills* offers a way to practice attention to what is, by encouraging you to reflect and observe within before engaging in a dialogue with another.

Attitude. Shapiro, et al. (2006) define attitude as those qualities a person brings to the act of attending to the present moment. The *footstep processes* of gaining perspective and empathy and compassion will result in a state of attending that is authentically engaged. This is in contrast to someone who uses attention merely to examine and critique a situation or person, resulting in a cold and aloof stance that may feel judgmental to those being observed. In effect, the authors posit that it is critical that one "consciously commits" to an attitude of compassion and empathy in conjunction with focusing upon your emotional experience. This is the ground upon which the *Touchstone Skills* and *footstep processes* are constructed as we learn to commit to an empathic and compassionate attitude toward ourselves and toward others.

Empowerment

Empowerment refers to the process by which you gain mastery of issues that are of concern. The empowerment process is defined as one that compels you, or the persons with whom you are affiliated, to take control over your lives. As such, it has much in common with Bandura's (1977) concepts of self-efficacy that refers to your expectations for success about situations that arise in your immediate or long-term future, due to your own efforts (Ries & Harter, 2012). An empowerment process encourages you to constructively release your own overt or dormant power and gain the skills and knowledge to overcome obstacles in your life. Ultimately, this should help you to develop and create change within yourself and in the lives of others, which is the ultimate goal of moving through the pathway.

Survey on Empowerment

1. One should not be too forward in terms of trying to make changes in a relationship,
It could be damaging.

☐ Very true (1) ☐ Sort of true (2) ☐ Not very true (3) ☐ Not at ALL true (4)

2. It is empowering to play a direct role in solving inevitable day-to-day problems in a relationship.

☐ Very true (4) ☐ Sort of true (3) ☐ Not very true (2) ☐ Not at ALL true (1)

3. One does not want to try to exercise power in a relationship because it upsets the balance.

☐ Very true (1) ☐ Sort of true (2) ☐ Not very true (3) ☐ Not at ALL true (4)

4. I feel confident in my ability to resolve dilemmas in a relationship by having a say in how we should proceed.

☐ Very true (4) ☐ Sort of true (3) ☐ Not very true (2) ☐ Not at ALL true (1)

Add up your four scores and divide by four. For a summary score, high scores mean high empowerment, low scores mean challenges to your sense of empowerment.

The Link Between Empowerment and Revealing Emotions

We have yoked these two concepts in this chapter for the following reasons. As we explained in presenting the *My Feelings* Survey, the emotions were presented in two groups. The first cluster of positive emotions we labeled as empowering emotions. This included: pride, gratefulness, happiness, contentment, empathy, and hopefulness. The second cluster of negative emotions we labeled disempowering emotions. These included: anger, guilt, anxiety, depression, humiliation, and despair. As you apply the *Touchstone Skills*, your goal is to increase the intensity of your empowering emotions and reduce the intensity of your disempowering emotions, which should facilitate the other *footstep processes* in toward resolution and self-liberation. For example, the first two steps of revealing emotions and general empowerment should make it more likely that you will be successful at the step of gaining perspective, appreciating your own perspective as well as that of others, and be better equipped to display the step of empathy and compassion. As we have described earlier in the text, this process should also facilitate your abilities to develop the final steps of transparency and authenticity, all processes that will also enhance the likelihood of resolution and self-liberation.

Moreover, the implications for our own view of empowering and disempowering emotions are clear. First, you must appreciate that you can experience emotions in both groups and that they do not represent an intractable duality of positive versus negative. Second, the balance of the positive or negative emotions is critical, and *can* be altered. In fact, the *Touchstone Skills* and the *footstep processes* are precisely designed to foster movement away from debilitating emotions toward the more empowering emotions. Although both positive and negative emotions may be experienced, if the balance can be shifted toward the more positive emotional pole, then less interpersonal distress will be experienced and there will be more room for negotiation around a mutually acceptable solution.

Case Scenario: The Plight of America's Wild Mustangs

We turn now to a dilemma that centers largely on differences in emotional reactions and levels of empowerment. These feelings were peaked because the people involved displayed a clash of values and beliefs. This dilemma has been modified for anonymity and is indirectly based on a Colorado news report, which recounts a growing divide about what to do about the burgeoning herds of wild horses that are creating stress on both the horses and on their environment. There are more than 37,000 wild horses (mustangs) and burros living freely on land owned by the state of Colorado. It is reported that these lands can only support an estimated 11,000 of these mustangs; therefore, there is growing pressure on the state from many interested groups to come up with a workable solution for this problem. The wild mustang problem ultimately falls on the shoulders of the state's Bureau of Land Management (BLM) and its advisory board members, who govern the lands the mustangs inhabit.

For purposes of this example, let's explore briefly the history and emotional reactivity of each camp regarding the mustangs. America's wild mustangs are spectacular to see, ranging in color and age, living wildly for centuries on the open plains and mountains of western America. They tend to represent a mythology of the old American west and its qualities of freedom, independence, and self-reliance. However, today these herds face famine from overpopulation and there is building resentment from local ranchers who perceive them as a threat to the precious grasslands intended to feed their cattle which, in turn, provides income for their families and community. For purposes of our story-line, we will address the dwindling funds to capture, auction, and warehouse these horses and the strong emotions evoked by competing needs. These competing needs are represented by: (1) the advisory board members of the Colorado Bureau of Land Management (BLM), (2) the ranchers, and (3) a local mustang advocacy group.

In our case scenario, the advisory board of the BLM intervened in the dilemma by appointing a wild horse specialist to help speak on their behalf and build consensus around how to deal with this growing problem. This specialist is a woman rancher and self-professed horse lover with a very pragmatic approach to this problem. However, she began her work by suggesting that the BLM consider the option of taking a certain portion of the mustangs to slaughter houses, which provoked strong emotions from the advocacy group that works to protect these animals. This led one faction of the BLM advisory board to oppose the specialist and take the option of putting the horses up for slaughter completely off the table. In the meantime, the mustang advocacy group, involved in the discussions, perceives that this specialist represents the cattle industry and believes she wants to pave the way for the slaughter of these animals. The BLM advisory board, now at arm's length from their appointed specialist, organized a daylong problem-solving meeting that included the three groups with differing positions (a) the BLM Specialist, (b) the head of the Mustang Advocacy Group, and (c) a representative of Western Colorado Ranchers Association.

The group met at the BLM headquarters in Colorado and, after introductions; they decided to spend some time sharing their perspectives and sentiments (feelings) about the mustang dilemma. The representative of the Western Ranchers Association shared first and talked about his anger at the consequences incurred by local ranchers when mustangs began encroaching more and more onto their grazing lands. "These horses are starving and their numbers are growing unchecked. It seems that every time the BLM comes up with a reasonable solution, some *Save the Mustang* advocacy group comes along and files an injunction. The Association is fed up and many members are threatening to start taking matters into their own hands by rounding up the mustangs and shooting them or hauling them up to Canada for slaughter."

The head of the Mustang advocacy group interrupted the representative's sharing, threatening, "That is a good way for a representative of the Ranchers' Association to end up in jail. These mustangs are protected by federal law and we will personally see that anyone who shoots at them goes to trial and perhaps prison." Her anger escalated and raising her voice she added, "What a bunch of barbarians you people are!" The Ranchers Association Representative, now frustrated, retorted, "You do-gooders think it is better to just let them starve to death? What kind of humane solution is that?" The head of the mustang Advocacy Group retorted, "You are both ranchers and your perspective is unduly influenced by your concern about how you can make money." At this point in the discussion, both groups were not only experiencing, but expressing, very strong disempowering emotions.

The wild horse Specialist stepped in and commented, "Both of you seem angry and frustrated about this dilemma and frankly, the BLM Advisory Board members share these sentiments. They also share a sense of guilt at having no clear answers for this situation. I think we should begin to explore options for the mustangs themselves rather than threaten and rail at one another. Why don't we try to shift this conversation to what we see happening and what we propose to do about it?" The representative of the Western Colorado Ranchers, now feeling more empowered, answered more calmly, "I hear you saying that we don't care about the horses and only about the money, but that is not true." He went on to re-frame, "My family has been involved in tilling this land for four generations, and we feel an obligation to the land and protecting it so that we can pass it on to many more future generations."

Empowered by the discussion, the representative continued, "When there were only a few thousand wild horses, we appreciated sharing the land with them. The mustangs reminded us of a time gone by when there were only open lands in the west and not as many competing pressures. Now, the situation has become desperate for us and for the horses as they face starvation. You would have to be completely heartless, not to feel for these suffering creatures." This dialogue, which began with the question, "Why don't we try to shift this conversation to what we see happening and what we propose to do about it?" began to edge the conversation away from revealing emotions to seeking empowerment through potential solutions.

After reflecting on the dialogue thus far, the BLM Specialist, in the spirit of what was now becoming a more transparent and authentic dialogue, began sharing her own feelings about the issue. "My overall concern is for these horses but I also have to consider the land and the local ranching communities and the policy of the Bureau of Land Management. Personally, I have been raising and training horses my entire life and I know them and love them like my own children. When I went up onto the mesa to check on the herd last week, I was depressed and wept as I rode along seeing the sick and dying horses, the newborns without mothers to nurse, and the males fighting for dominance in a way much more violent than in the past when they were well fed. I did not come here to take any sides but to state my understanding (compassion and empathy) for the Advisory Board of the BLM, yet highlight that what they are doing is not working and it is mostly not helping these magnificent wild creatures. When the question was posed 'who cares about the mustangs' I thought to myself 'we all do'. That is why I want each of us to share and explore solutions as a team."

The representative from the Rancher's Association concurred, "I had to call the BLM last month because a young Mustang was lying down next to my property. It was just a bag of bones and I know that starvation is a terrible and painful way to die for any animal. There has to be some way to help these horses without all of this contentious fighting." Revealing disempowering emotions and sharing perspectives continued to empower the group as they moved the discussion forward. They began to more carefully reflect back each other's statements, creating the opportunity to reframe the overarching dilemma into a problem-solving statement, where each had power to join together in the best interests for the mustangs. This ongoing process of reframing gave way to hope and empathy that if they were to work as a team, the mustangs might be saved from slaughter on one extreme and starvation on the other.

The head of the Mustang Advocacy Group began to engage from a more transparent and authentic stance with the BLM Specialist and the representative of the Western Colorado Ranchers by saying, "I am surprised to hear you talk about the horses this way. Some of the members of each of your groups have made some pretty insensitive accusations about the horses in the newspapers. Just last week a rancher argued that every Mustang should be hunted down and shot or sent to slaughter." The BLM Specialist apologized for her initial call for slaughtering the horses, remarking that she spoke too quickly and should have spent more time researching the issue before saying anything publically. She reassured the head of the Mustang Advocacy Group that the BLM Advisory Board had a no-kill policy with regard to the Mustangs. On the other hand, the Specialist shared concern that thousands of the horses were now confined to small pens until they were adopted. "Many of them won't be adopted, so they will spend the rest of their lives in twenty-four square feet pens. This is against everything in their nature, and although it is better than starvation or slaughter, it is not a long term solution.

As you can see from the conversation thus far, the three parties have revealed their emotions about the horses and they were united by similar feelings of anger, frustration and despair over the fate of the mustangs. Through the *Touchstone Skills*, they moved into empowerment about the dilemma and each began to share their unique perspectives providing the others with an opportunity to see the situation from their unique vantage point. They slowly began to gain perspective on the situation by broadening their own view, sharing it, and then adopting subtle perspective-shifts in how they saw not only the situation but the compassion of the people involved.

The head of the Mustang Advocacy Group began to have empathy for the BLM Specialist and sees her as an advocate for the horses and the leader of the Advocacy Group also was struck by the representative of Western Colorado Ranchers despair and guilt over witnessing the starving horse. The representative of Western Colorado Ranchers began to see that, although the head of the Mustang Advocacy Group presented real roadblocks to progress, members of his group were inflaming the situation by making arguments that did not represent the view of the Ranchers Association as a whole. Through questioning, reflecting and reframing skills, they each moved from sharing their own perspective to understanding each other's vantage point and each began a real shift away from their personal agendas, leading to greater compassion and empathy for one another's position. Ultimately they created a joint statement of resolution that began with, "How do we collaborate to help our wild mustangs?" Their increased compassion for one another resulted in a shift from their negative emotional states to more positive, empowering emotions. This created more transparency as they began to question, reflect, and reframe more openly with one another about possible options for the mustangs. The representative of Western Colorado Ranchers shared that he had to answer to the Rancher's Association and, although they were pretty moderate, some more extreme members were gaining ground because no workable solution had been found. The head of the Mustang Advocacy Group also shared that she did not want to just throw up roadblocks but come up with a reasonable resolution to this dilemma. She had some extreme people in her group that were willing to say "no" to everything except the status quo. The BLM Specialist also said the BLM advisory board was in a real fix as funds were dwindling and they were spending far too much money on this one program while others were badly underfunded. This transparent and authentic sharing allowed each of them to feel a growing sense that they were collectively in this dilemma together and had to find a way out as a group. They agreed to spend the rest of the day brain storming any and every option they could think of, where the overall interest was ultimately how to save the wild horses, while preserving the land.

In the daylong meeting, each group felt more empowered and resolution was reached in terms of two key issues. The three agreed to speak with their constituents about allocating funds they had been using to lobby and fight one another and instead devote these monies to programs that would address the situation directly. They also agreed to help the BLM rewrite wild horse adoption rules so it would be easier for people to adopt a wild mustang while making it harder for those that used adoption to secretly take them for slaughter. They each agreed to remain team players with regard to this ongoing dilemma even though realistically they also had to answer to the different needs of each of their constituents.

In the *My Feelings* Survey presented earlier in this chapter, you may remember that the emotions were displayed in two groups: empowering and disempowering. The empowering group of positive emotions included pride, gratefulness, happiness, contentment, empathy, and hopefulness. The second cluster of disempowering emotions included anger, guilt, anxiety, depression, humiliation, and despair. When you examine the emotions of the people described in the case scenario, you can see that they began the meeting from the disempowering cluster, which is why it is was initially very difficult for them to create a solution. In a sense, this common ground of disempowerment allowed them to connect on an emotional level even though it began combatively. As the meeting, progressed, these shared feelings of anger and frustration allowed them to appreciate that they each wanted to take more empowering action to solve the dilemma.

The *Touchstone Skills* and the *footstep processes* are precisely designed to foster movement away from debilitating emotions toward the more empowering emotions. Although both positive and negative emotions may be experienced, if the balance can be shifted toward the more positive emotional pole, then less interpersonal distress will be experienced. Once this shift begins, there is more room for negotiation around a mutually acceptable solution as individuals and groups gain mastery over issues of concern to them, which is the very essence of empowerment. The goal of using the *Touchstone Skills* is to increase the intensity of the empowering emotions and reduce the intensity of the disempowering emotions, which should facilitate the other stepping stones in the circle to peaceful resolution. Empowerment and empowering emotions should make it more likely that you will gain perspective, appreciating your own as well as others, and be better equipped to display empathy and compassion. As we have described earlier in the text, this should also facilitate your abilities to develop transparency and authenticity, all processes that will enhance the likelihood of your obtaining change in resolving the dilemma. In the next chapter, we turn to the third and fourth of these footsteps: gaining perspective and developing empathy and compassion.

Chapter Four
Gaining Perspective, Compassion and Empathy

Overview

At this point, you have set your intention to learn how to communicate more clearly and understand how to intervene in order to quiet any negative self-talk that might interfere with this intention. As part of this process, you have started to become more familiar with the *Touchstone Skills* and *footstep processes*, helping you to begin to apply the next first two footsteps of revealing emotions and empowerment to communication. This chapter begins by illustrating the next two important steps of gaining perspective and developing empathy and compassion. Each of the footsteps to self-liberation concludes with a survey that allows you to measure your level of comfort with these processes. The chapter ends with a demonstration of how these concepts become integrated into a case scenario involving two parents and their adolescent children.

Gaining Perspective

Gaining perspective involves three components: *perspective-taking, perspective-sharing* and *perspective shifting*. Perspective-taking on an intra-psychic level simply means stepping back and understanding your personal historical beliefs and experiences that form your current perspective. This allows for greater receptivity to the views and beliefs of another person based on their own experiences. Perspective-sharing is an interpersonal process whereby you share your point of view with another. Perspective-shifting occurs when you, the other or both of you, alter your perspectives based on perspective sharing.

Gaining perspective is the foundation for the next footstep of developing compassion and empathy, because when you suspend your judgment and open to the perspectives of another, you naturally increase your compassion and empathy for them. Empathy and compassion are different from pity, which involves feeling sorry for someone's plight without engaging in an understanding of their situation or perspective. We posit that along the pathway, you continually deepen your capacity for the cultivation of compassion and empathy. This impacts and enriches the experience, not only the relationships in which conflict is currently being experienced, but also for everyone with whom you interact, whether it is the person checking out your groceries or your closest friends and family members.

Perspective-Taking: Mine, Yours and Theirs

Understanding the perspective of the self and others is a powerful, and often elusive, human cognition, because it is essentially a result of one's personal opinion and belief system. Differing motivations, expectations, knowledge, or even one's visual perspective can lead people to interpret the same event very differently. Thus, a failure to recognize these differences may lead to miscommunication, dilemmas and conflict (e.g., Pronin, Puccio, & Ross, 2002). Many argue that the correctness of their perspective is predicated on a thorough review of the facts. Yet, facts are often selected on the basis of one's personal biases and considerations that support one's own perspective. Oftentimes, in the legal profession you will hear the response "It depends." to a specific question asked because one's perspective informs such a response. It depends on the perspective of the judge, or it depends on the nature of the opposing party. Or it depends on the vantage point of a specific leader of a particular government, organization or family and the history and experience that informed their perspective. Eventually, it becomes difficult to determine which came first, the supposed facts or the perspective. This is reminiscent of the historical debate about whether thoughts or emotions occur first. The answer is, "It depends."

Business management consultant David Allen (2008) notes that perspective has a direct relationship to the level of control one has over one's life. Someone with disorganized thinking or a disorganized and chaotic life can easily lose the ability to see beyond the chaos. In the intense stress of conflict, this chaos may escalate creating even greater drama and panic. As he notes, "Perspective is the key, but it is a very slippery commodity. It can be lost in an instant (2008, p. 45)." Perhaps, Anais Nin best described perspective by noting that we don't see things as they are, we see them as we are.

Piaget and the Origins of Perspective-Taking

Piaget (1960) was recognized as one of the intellectual giants of the twentieth century, due to his extensive contributions to the field of cognitive development. In addition to his well-known stage model of development, he addressed numerous other developmental constructs, one of which was perspective-taking. As the name implies, this process addresses an individual's ability to take the perspective of another person, to see things from his or her point of view. Piaget's contribution was to explore the developmental trajectory of *spatial* perspective-taking that occurs in young children. The absence of this perspective-taking ability was viewed as a manifestation of egocentrism.

Living in Geneva, surrounded by mountains in the distance, Piaget capitalized on the fact that mountains would be familiar landmarks for children. Thus, to examine spatial perspective taking, he constructed a replica of a mountain, about three feet in diameter, the various faces of which differed in the same manner as the actual mountains. The mock mountain was placed on a small table and the child was invited to slowly walk around the table concentrating on what the mountain looked like on all sides. The child then returned to the starting point, and Piaget sat across from the child and asked, "Tell me what the mountain looks like from where I am sitting across from you. Describe what *I* see." Very young children (ages 3-5) were unable to answer the question correctly, even though they had walked around the mountain and examined all sides. They described their own perspective, what they saw directly in front of them, which was their own egocentric view of the mountain, not Piaget's view. Older children, were able to successfully understand the task and could psychologically put themselves in the position of Piaget's spatial perception of the mountain by recalling what they had observed when they walked around the mountain.

Others in the developmental psychology field extended the concept to *cognitive* perspective-taking. They wanted to know to what extent an individual might understand what another is thinking. This is a more complex developmental task because it involves more challenging demands that were no longer supported by physical or spatial clues. One had to get into the mind of another. Subsequent investigators further expanded the concept to the domain of *emotional* perspective-taking, which represents an even more advanced set of skills requiring empathy for another's inner feelings which may or may not be expressed explicitly. (For the reader interested in how egocentrism and perspective-taking emerge over childhood and adolescence, see Harter, 2013).

One of the challenges to both cognitive and emotional perspective-taking is that certain dynamics, first identified by Freud, can interfere, notably projection, which we described briefly in Chapter One. In this case, rather than truly understanding another person's point of view or actually empathizing with his or her position, we project our own interpretation of what we would think or feel in a similar situation. In this sense, projection represents an adult form of egocentrism. We can see the analogy to Piaget's observations of how young children egocentrically project their perceptions of their own spatial perspective of the mountain onto the other person, rather than appreciating that the other person has a different point of view.

Piaget and others demonstrated that the ability to see the world from the perspective of another is a developmental movement from the more egocentric child to the higher social functioning of an adult. However, the authors (Epley, Morewedge, & Boyaz) of a 2003 study from Harvard University posit, that although adults do appear to be less egocentric than children, these differences may be produced by "differences in the ability to correct an initial egocentric interpretation, rather than differences in the tendency to form one."(p. 760). The authors note that adults continue some manner of child-like thinking through a wide variety of social judgments that are egocentrically biased. Indeed, they argue that our adult tendencies such as overestimating the extent to which others share our own attitudes and feelings demonstrate that "egocentrism is not merely a passing phase of childhood, but a fact of life" (p. 761).

The cognitive-developmental literature broadens the approach to egocentrism by revealing new forms of adolescent egocentrism (Elkind 1967, Piaget 1960). The first of these forms Elkind refers to as the *personal fable*, which can be represented by the statement, "I am so unique no one else can possibly understand my perspective. I'm invincible. I'm special." In this case, you might lose the sense that someone else can ever understand your point of view. For example, you might exclaim that, "No one else can possibly understand what it is like to be in love." Elkind referred to the second type of adolescent egocentrism as the *imaginary audience*, where you might assume that others are as preoccupied or as interested in your situation as you are. An example may be the thought that, "Everyone in the stadium is looking at me when I go to a football game; they are all staring at how I am dressed." Either of these forms can interfere with the three components of gaining perspective (a) perspective-taking; (b) perspective-sharing; and (c) perspective-shifting.

How is this historical foray into the origins of concepts about gaining perspective relevant to the *Touchstones Skills* described in this book? If egocentrism alters its nature over the course of development and takes on new forms, then the need for expanded ways to correct self-centered interpretations is a necessity on the pathway to authentic communication. Certain adults, under stress, may regress under unique circumstances to forms of adolescent egocentrism. A major goal of our book is to help you create ever expanding skills and concepts that will promote authentic communication, constantly improving your perspective-taking. The purpose of revealing emotions, critical on your pathway, is the acknowledging of your feelings to the other person, as honestly and genuinely as possible, so that they can appreciate your perspective. Opening this dialogue promotes perspective-sharing, which, in turn, provides an opportunity to engage in empathy and compassion. This then leads to what we have coined perspective-shifting, providing the momentum to engage the *Touchstone Skills* of questioning, reflecting, and reframing foundational in order to gain a new perspective.

A Return to Empathy and Compassion

As the pathway reveals, the results of such emotional and cognitive perspective-taking, perspective-sharing and perspective-shifting can lead to empathy and a more compassionate understanding of the other person's point of view. Before we introduce two surveys for you to measure your current abilities with these two footsteps, it may be helpful to review what we mean by empathy and compassion. Empathy, as we defined it in Chapter One, aligns with Batson's (2009) concept of this as the ability or process of imagining how another person is thinking and feeling. In this definition, empathy "is measured by one's sensitivity to the way the other is affected by his or her situation" (p.7). To reiterate, Barrett-Lennard (1981) referred to this as adopting an "empathic attentional set" that involves "a process of feeling into, in which Person A opens him-or herself- in a deeply responsive way to Person B's feelings and experiencing but without losing awareness that B is a distinct other self" (p. 92). We defined *compassion* as the deeper emotional component of perspective-shifting, where your awareness shifts to a more expansive desire to alleviate another person's suffering. Casell (2002) makes the important point that you must perceive a shared sense of community with others in order to feel true compassion. Without this, we tend to alienate or dissociate ourselves from those less fortunate.

The following two surveys are provided for you to measure your current levels of ability in taking in the perspectives of others and in developing empathy and compassion. Again, we invite you to record your responses and then return again later to take the survey again and see if there has been a change.

Survey on Perspective-taking

1. I find it hard to take another person's perspective because I usually feel that mine is more accurate.

☐ Very true (1) ☐ Sort of true (2) ☐ Not very true (3) ☐ Not at ALL true (4)

2. It is important to appreciate another's point of view even if there is a difference of opinion.

☐ Very true (4) ☐ Sort of true (3) ☐ Not very true (2) ☐ Not at ALL true (1)

3. Understanding another person's viewpoint is difficult for me, because, I would rather they see the world the way I see it.

☐ Very true (1) ☐ Sort of true (2) ☐ Not very true (3) ☐ Not at ALL true (4)

4. Seeing things from another's vantage point helps me think out of the box and ultimately improves my communication within a relationship.

☐ Very true (4) ☐ Sort of true (3) ☐ Not very true (2) ☐ Not at ALL true (1)

Add up your scores and divide by four. The higher the total score, the better your perspective-taking. Lower scores reflect challenges to your perspective-taking abilities.

Survey on Feelings of Empathy and Compassion

1. I don't see how feeling empathy for another person will help me better communicate with them.

☐ Very true (1) ☐ Sort of true (2) ☐ Not very true (3) ☐ Not at ALL true (4)

2. It strikes me that being empathic toward another is a basic human value that would improve any relationship.

☐ Very true (4) ☐ Sort of true (3) ☐ Not very true (2) ☐ Not at ALL true (1)

3. I don't see how compassion would help me understand another person's perspective more easily.

☐ Very true (1) ☐ Sort of true (2) ☐ Not very true (3) ☐ Not at ALL true (4)

4. I believe that the desire to alleviate another person's suffering can allow me to more fully appreciate their perspective, even if it is very different from my own.

☐ Very true (4) ☐ Sort of true (3) ☐ Not very true (2) ☐ Not at ALL true (1)

Sum your four scores and divide by 4. A higher average score represents greater empathy and compassion. A lower score represents a challenge in displaying these skills.

Case Scenario: The Family Vacation

There are many issues and day-to-day decisions within every family that must be resolved in order to maintain the smooth functioning of the family unit. These decisions include substantial choices, for instance, where to live and the many factors that affect this choice such as what the school system is like, safety and comfort of the new city, size and cost of the home, and proximity to work. It also includes a myriad of other less gripping decisions, for example what kind of car or appliance to purchase, where to go on the family vacation, or more common day-to-day decisions around household management, such as who does what chores, shopping, meal preparation, laundry, and transportation of children. Our case scenario, presented next, provides a backdrop for scholarly work on family communication and its connection to perspective taking, empathy and compassion, while providing specific application of the *Touchstone Skills* to a family decision making process.

Autonomy and Connectedness. Cooper, Grotevant, & Condon (1983) presented a model of family communication patterns demonstrating how the communication patterns of parents filter down to their adolescents, either facilitating or compromising their adolescents' perspective-taking abilities and their ability to explore different alternatives for their future. We will weave their research and theory into a case study demonstrating the use of the *Touchstone Skills*, both intra-psychically and interpersonally. In so doing, we will demonstrate how certain parental communication patterns can enhance a child's use of the skills and how this relates to the development of gaining perspective and empathy and compassion.

As any parent can attest, adolescence is a stage in development that can create many new dilemmas and issues which can dissolve quickly into conflict. Parents need not only the skills to communicate effectively but demonstrate the ability to show empathy for the developmental needs of their rapidly changing teenagers. In recent years, the field of developmental psychology has shifted from an emphasis solely on independence or autonomy as a primary goal of development, to a realization that the most adaptive stance is to combine both autonomy and connectedness to others, rather than viewing them as contradictory. We see this trend among those addressing issues in infancy, childhood, adolescence, and adulthood (see Harter, 1999, for a review of this literature). The American cultural emphasis on individuality makes this balancing act more difficult, not only for adolescents but for all family members.

Cooper and colleagues (1983) tackle this issue within the context of parents with adolescents because the task during this period is not just to obtain psychological autonomy and individuate from parents, but to also remain connected to parents and family. It is a dual task and tensions often rise when trying to negotiate what seem like contradictory goals. The authors demonstrate that two particular parenting communication skills, what they term *individuality* and *connectedness*, can dramatically impact this difficult time in adolescent development. They divide the individuality communication style into two sub-categories of (1) self-assertion, which is the ability to have and communicate a point of view, and (2) separateness, which is the use of communication patterns that express how one's views may be separate from others. They argue that a parent must be able to actively and clearly communicate differences of viewpoint and opinion from those held by their adolescent, in order to serve as a role model who nurtures individuation for their adolescent.

97

Cooper and colleagues note that individuality is not a sufficient communication process in and of itself. It must include two dimensions of connectedness, (1) openness to the perspectives of others, and (2) mutuality, which is the respect and support of others' opinions, even if there is disagreement. This type of communication style invites both empathy and compassion into a dialogue as the parents communicate their respect for their adolescents' opinions, even if they do not agree. The authors argue that the more all family members are involved in a dilemma, the more likely they will be able to achieve a desirable, mutual outcome. In their research, they relate the parents' styles of communication to their adolescents' ability to take the perspective of another and to explore their own identity.

Cooper and colleagues created a research model, which we will use as the basis for our family case study. In this research, families were invited to their laboratory to discuss a family vacation, creating a mock kitchen table setting. On this hypothetical vacation, the family must discuss together where do they want to go, why, for how long, under what circumstances, and what will they gain, learn, and enjoy. All family members, a mother, father, and typically two adolescents, are free to openly discuss these issues. The authors do not frame this process as a conflict but as a decision-making task on the part of the family.

Family Communication Differences. Our case scenario will demonstrate how different communication styles dictate different outcomes and how important the *Touchstone Skills* are in each communication style. Listening and reflecting skills, perspective-taking, perspective-sharing, and perspective shifting skills are critical elements of this decision making process as is the concept of transparency, wherein parental messages are communicated in a manner that is clearly stated, including how the parents' views might be different from that of the adolescent (the concept of separateness). However, as Cooper and colleagues note, these messages of individuality and differentiation must be combined with the concept of connectedness. For instance, the parents, in this case, must be open to the view of their adolescents; they must listen, and be sensitive and respectful of their adolescents' point of view, which naturally demonstrates compassion and empathy.

In this research model, Cooper and her colleagues identified combinations of the two parental communication forms of individuality and connectedness, which have implications for the specific use of the *Touchstone Skills*. They identified the following four combinations of parenting communication styles; (1) high on both individuality and connectedness, (2) high on individuality but low on connectedness, (3) high on connectedness, but low on individuality, and (4) low on both individuality and connectedness.

How might these combinations play out, in terms of the implications for the *Touchstone Skills*, as applied to their family vacation planning scenario? Let us first consider those parents who are high on individuality and express their own perspectives clearly and are also high on connectedness, exemplified by their openness to the views of their adolescent children (perspective sharing). In this case, individuality is directly relevant to the concept of empowerment, in that adolescents can explore and voice their own point of view. This stance would allow the adolescents to exercise the *Touchstone Skills* of questioning their parent's position and reflecting on the various alternative perspectives. Because, they believe their parents listen to them, they will be in a position to reframe their own initial thinking and shift perspectives in the service of the higher value of harmony within the family.

Obviously, this style of parental communication is the ideal for successfully using the *Touchstone Skills* and *footstep processes;* however, the other three combinations of communication could certainly all benefit by employing these skills and concepts. A family high on individuality and low on connectedness might very well experience a shift to greater connectedness through the consistent use of the skills of questioning, reflecting, and reframing. Certainly, a family high on connectedness but low on autonomy might learn to shift this stance as they practiced skills that required them to listen to one another's opinions and explore them with reflection and reframing. Even a family whose communication patterns are low on both individuality and connectedness might experience a larger measure of both through the use of skills that join them in a common goal and listen, even in the most rudimentary way, to views with which they may not agree. For now, we assume that the following family is high on both individuality and connectedness and take them through the *Touchstone Skills*, concentrating on their questions and statements in each category.

Intra-psychic questioning by parents. The parents in this case would begin the process by asking themselves a series of questions such as, "How do I really feel about a family vacation? "Well, on the one hand, I am happy, if not elated, that the kids would want to be with us for that long, at their age. However, I also don't want to be disappointed, guilty, or even depressed, if the vacation does not go well." Other questions followed including, "Just what can we afford in the way of a vacation for the entire family, given our budget constraints?" "Do we have enough experience or knowledge about how to meet everyone's needs?" "What do we envision in terms of the ideal outcome of such a vacation?"

Intra-psychic questioning by adolescents. Each adolescent may also first privately considered a set of questions such as, "Do I really think this will be a happy time for me, should I feel hopeful? I mean, sometimes I think my parents don't understand what it is like to be a teenager. So will I feel angry and guilty for suggesting such an idea in the first place?" "Do I really want to spend two weeks with my family and be away from my friends during summer break?" "Two weeks is an eternity!" "I don't think a family vacation will include what I want to do but more what they want." "How much 'say' will I really have in the planning? I'm just a kid, so won't I have to do what my parents really want?"

Intra-psychic reflecting by parents. A parent may engage in an internal dialogue reflecting on the wisdom of taking the entire family on a vacation together. "I must admit, I am not always at my best when it comes to setting up a realistic budget." "We need to set some initial constraints on how much we can spend." "We really must think through how to meet everyone's needs, given how different each of our interests are."

Intra-psychic reflecting by adolescents. Each adolescent needs to reflect upon the issues raised by the questioning phase. "I guess I could be away from my friends, maybe text them every day, to stay in touch." "If it is truly a family decision, then I probably shouldn't worry too much about whether I will have a good time and just see what happens."

Intra-psychic reframing by parents. A parent might reframe any anxieties they express by saying "I'm a responsible parent, I can certainly pull it together to come up with a reasonable budget that we can stick to, if we are clear at the outset." "We want to be sure that we pick a place where everyone's different needs and interests can be met. So as a parent, I need to think this through and do some research on possible options and what they might have to offer, before we have our family discussion." "The kids are older now, so we might be able to select a vacation where it would be safe to let them do some things on their own."

Intra-psychic-reframing by adolescents. An adolescent intra-psychic reframe might include, "It may be good to be away from my friends for a couple of weeks; after all, it's not the end of the world. Maybe I'll even make some new friends." "Maybe I'll have some interesting experiences to share with my friends, though I sort of doubt it." "I know I want to be on my own this summer but there aren't too many summers left for family trips before I leave for college. I have enjoyed the other trips we made together; I just want to make sure there are things for me to do on my own."

Each family member brings his or her own intra-psychic questions, reflections, and reframes to the family kitchen table discussion, to plan the anticipated vacation. Before they used the three skills, they agreed to share what they were feeling about the situation. The parents talked about their anxiety over money and that the trip would end up not being good for the family budget. They also shared their sadness that there were probably not too many of these trips ahead now that the kids were close to leaving home. The children shared their frustration of having to leave their friends over the summer and their fear that the trip would be boring. They all agreed that the best way to explore these emotions and become more empowered about the trip was to take some time to really listen to one another's needs. At this point, they started their interpersonal use of the *Touchstone Skills*.

Interpersonal questioning by parents. "Before we go overboard in our planning, guys, we first need to ask how much money it would take to go where we would like to go." "We also need to ask what would be fun for each of us to do, what would be fair given our different interests?" "And then there is the question of keeping in touch with your friends?" "So let's start there, and together discuss and try to answer these questions."

Interpersonal questioning by adolescents. "I also thought about how we all have such different interests. Where could we possibly go so that everyone would be pretty happy with our choice?" "I suppose I could stay in touch with my friends, maybe even a couple of phone calls on my cell phone, if I did not use too many minutes. Mom and Dad, could that work out?"

Interpersonal reflecting by parents. "These are good questions that we are each bringing to the table. Let's reflect on everyone's wishes and concerns." "We do have to be careful about money and set some kind of budget, for the family as a whole, and for each one of us. So we want to share with you what we can afford." "You kids have different interests and we have our own interests as well. Let's spend some time sharing what those are." "Maybe there are some common interests we could enjoy, and if we pick the right place, everyone might get to enjoy a few of their interests." "Let's think more about how to make sure that you kids can stay in touch with your friends, we hear how important that is to you."

Interpersonal reflecting by adolescents. "Those sound like good ideas, and we totally get the money thing." "I like your idea about finding some place to go, where there are some things that we could all do together, but other activities we could do on our own, since we have such different interests." "I'm glad you hear how important it is to be able to stay in touch with my friends, too. I want to go someplace that will make them all jealous!"

Interpersonal reframing by parents. "We have done some preliminary budgeting so that as a family, this would not be an outrageous expense, because we have to be realistic, and we are glad that you kids appreciate that. We want you to grow up to be responsible managers of your own money. How about if you do more chores around the house and we increase your allowance, so you will have some vacation money?" "We want to make sure that everyone has as much fun as possible, since this *is* a vacation, we want to respect everyone's interests." "So, we did some research on the internet. We thought a trip to San Diego might fit the bill." "Perhaps we could cut the vacation to 10 days rather than two weeks. That will help with the budget and make sure we don't make the trip too long." "We found a great deal on flights and on a rental car and house that is near the beach." "San Diego has enough things going on that we could all find things to do together and apart. For instance, we could go sailing as a family, you kids could learn to surf, and we could go out by ourselves at night for dinner and dancing." "San Diego is only one idea but we wanted to present it to you so you can see that we can find a place that all of us would enjoy."

Interpersonal reframing by adolescents. "Wow, surfing, that would be so cool and my friends will be so jealous!" "I had an idea about money, maybe I could get a job in the neighborhood for the beginning of the summer, to save up some money that would help out. That way, I could afford to call my friends and have spending cash for the trip. And, if we are only going to be away for 10 days, I think I will probably survive!" The other adolescent was not so interested in surfing but said that sailing sounds fun and so did just reading on the beach. She commented, "I know it is two years away, but can I look at Scripps Institute for oceanography? It would be cool to see that school and I would love to go whale watching if they are there that time of year."

This case scenario represents a very high functioning family where all the members are relatively comfortable expressing both their need for autonomy and for connectedness. They have a history of communicating in this manner which makes the family vacation dilemma easy to discuss and resolve. However, this is not to say that families with greater communication challenges could not benefit from the *Touchstone Skills* and *footstep processes*. Because the pathway is cyclical, anyone can begin immediately using the skills and processes without understanding all the nuances. Each time this kind of action is initiated, the entire pathway is illuminated and positively affected by the change, no matter how small or measured.

In this chapter, we illustrated how emotions enhance your perception and understanding of events, other people, and the world in general and how emotions that are empowering, can help you move along the path. Additionally, we demonstrated that learning to take the perspectives of another promotes the development of empathy and compassion, which broadens your ability to take in and appreciate even more diverse perspectives. Compassion and empathy, in turn, lead to greater transparency, which allows for greater authenticity, which comprise the final two footsteps, covered in the next chapter.

Chapter Five
Transparency and Authenticity

Overview

This chapter presents the final two *footstep processes* of transparency and authenticity, which are often linked together in their application and intent. Transparency is the practice of making the covert more overt by bringing emotions and thoughts into conscious awareness in a manner that is genuine. Harter (2012) defines genuineness or authenticity as acting and expressing oneself in ways that are consistent with inwardly experienced values, desires, and emotions. In a sense, this translates to having congruency between what you think and feel and how you act and express yourself outwardly.

We will begin this chapter with the concept of transparency, followed by a survey in which you can measure your current ability to be transparent. We follow this brief overview of transparency with a more in depth look at authenticity, which has a longer tradition of research and writing within the field of psychology and related disciplines. At the conclusion of this discussion, you will have an opportunity to complete a survey on your own perceptions of how authenticity operates in your life. The chapter concludes with a workplace case scenario that demonstrates the use of the *Touchstone Skills* and how they relate to transparency and authenticity.

The Importance of Transparency

Transparency, in regard to authenticity, means to express yourself in a manner that can be readily understood, accessible, and free from pretense or deception. We invite you to let transparency refer to how you incorporate self-knowledge in ways that create greater understanding of your own being and your relation to others. It is what philosopher Eugene Halliday (1989) referred to as the development of a reflexive self-consciousness, one that is both self-transparent and also aware of its presence in the natural world. Halliday notes that we can promote a more spontaneous form of awareness by turning our own consciousness back onto itself and become the observing self that is at the core of mindfulness. He sees this as a method that leads to self-liberation, whereby we break the cycle of conditioned reflexes, habitually driving us in pursuit of pleasure and avoidance of pain.

What do we mean when we speak of habitual thinking and conditioned reflexes? Much of the study of these processes comes from the field of psychology. Although Freud has been criticized for many of his ideas, his study of habitual unconscious responses is still very useful today. For example, Freud (1952) illuminated the distinction between conscious and unconscious mental processes, identifying numerous unconscious *defense* mechanisms. We have touched on two of these in Chapter One, *projection,* which is displacing your negative feelings onto others and *reaction formation,* defined as reacting against a tendency you see in others that is unconsciously something in yourself. Here we add a third defense that Freud termed *introjection,* whereby you identify strongly with an idea or person to the point that it becomes a part of your own belief system. These defense mechanisms along with other negative cycles of misperception confuse our thinking and lead to faulty conclusions because they interfere with accurate reality testing.

The practice of the *Touchstone Skills* will help you uncover these unconscious processes through the consistent mindful practice of questioning why you are experiencing certain feelings and thoughts, reflecting back these thoughts and feelings to bring those more to conscious awareness, and reframing the negative misperceptions into thoughts and feelings that will help you develop greater internal balance. With time and practice, these skills and processes will become second nature to you, helping you respond with greater flexibility to everyday dilemmas and more acute conflicts by reducing habitual responses that spring from past hurts or rigid interpretations.

Survey on Transparency

1. I shouldn't be too open about sharing my thoughts and feelings in a relationship; it can make me very vulnerable.

☐ Very true (1) ☐ Sort of true (2) ☐ Not very true (3) ☐ Not at ALL true (4)

2. I like the idea of being open and honest in a relationship, although I need some additional skills to make this happen.

☐ Very true (4) ☐ Sort of true (3) ☐ Not very true (2) ☐ Not at ALL true (1)

3. I believe one can be a little too transparent in a relationship, letting it all hang out.

☐ Very true (1) ☐ Sort of true (2) ☐ Not very true (3) ☐ Not at ALL true (4)

4. Communicating honestly, openly, and transparently in a relationship can only serve to enhance a relationship, bringing greater authenticity.

☐ Very true (4) ☐ Sort of true (3) ☐ Not very true (2) ☐ Not at ALL true (1)

Add up your four scores and divide by four. High scores mean high transparency, low scores indicate challenges to transparency.

Authenticity

Authenticity, namely, the ability to speak and act in accord with one's true inner self, is relevant to many of the principles that guide the practice of the *Touchstone Skills* and the *footstep processes*. Authenticity is associated with many indices of positive mental health, such as optimal and realistically positive self-esteem; more adaptive decision-making and life choices; more appropriate mastery and problem-solving investments; and improved interpersonal relationships (Harter, 2012). Therefore, our central thesis is that the general principles espoused by the *InAccord* model, as well as its specific *Touchstone Skills*, have been developed to foster authenticity. In the book, *In Justice, InAccord* (Ries & Harter, 2012), the authors applied these general principles and skills to those who seek mediation in order to resolve interpersonal disputes and conflicts. *Touchstones* broadens the applicability of these principles and skills in order to promote positive outcomes in people's lives, especially given the everyday interpersonal challenges that require thoughtful, authentic communication and shared decision-making efforts.

In the following pages, we will illustrate the developmental roots of authenticity. These begin to take hold in adolescence, many times painfully, as teenagers become consciously aware of contradictions between how they act and respond differently with parents, friends, and teachers. During late adolescent and early adulthood, we learn to abstract and normalize experiences and become more aware and accommodating of the ways we respond to different groups and individuals. This is also a time where we easily succumb to the pressures of others and of our culture, which may support the development of barriers to our authenticity such as self-distorting behaviors and negative, or false, self-talk. We will present some of these barriers in this section along with ways to mitigate the barriers through new behaviors and habits. These include greater transparency, better listening skills with self and others, techniques to quiet the ego, such as mindfulness and humility, and the development of dispositional authenticity that includes increased self-awareness, realistic self-appraisals, congruence, relational honesty, openness, and genuineness.

Developmental Roots of Authenticity

Research in developmental psychology has shown that an awareness of the false self-behavior of others, and eventually the self, becomes particularly acute beginning in mid-adolescence (Harter, Bresnick, Bouchey, & Whitesell, 1997.) It is here that terms such as being "phony" become prevalent in the language of teenagers. Initially, there may be accusations that others are being hypocrites, followed by a budding realization that they, themselves, are not saying what they really believe or are merely saying what they think someone else wants to hear. The detection of deception, first in others, but eventually in them, emerges as a highly salient preoccupation in adolescents' thinking and vocabulary.

Just why should the period of mid-adolescence become particularly problematic in terms of the emergence of a concern with false self-behavior and one's authenticity? During adolescence, the self becomes increasingly more differentiated, that is, one constructs a self with one's parents, a self with one's friends, a self as a student in the classroom, a self in budding romantic relationships, and a self at a job. These differentiated selves do not always speak with one voice. In fact, these selves may become quite inconsistent. For example, an adolescent may admit, "I am depressed with my parents, rowdy with peers, caring with close friends, pretty studious in the classroom, self-conscious in a romantic relationship, and responsible at my after-school job." So, how are these disparate role-related selves to be coordinated, how are potential contradictions to be resolved, and what are the implications for the development of true versus false self-behavior? A 20-year program of research has revealed some fascinating findings (Harter et al., 1997).

During mid-adolescence, there is a cognitive explosion of new skills that can be applied to many domains, including the self (Fischer, 1980; Harter, 1999; Harter, 2012), but not without liabilities. Adolescents eventually develop the cognitive ability to simultaneously compare and contrast the characteristics that define their multiple selves and, as a result, they are able to detect major inconsistencies. For example, they observe that they may be cheerful with friends and depressed with parents. Yet how can this possibly be, they ponder, since these are so contradictory?

The construction and recognition of contradictory attributes across one's multiple selves understandably provokes a concern over which of these opposing characteristics reflects one's "true" versus one's "false" self. The twenty-year study revealed that it is not uncommon for those in mid-adolescence to spontaneously agonize over just which features of their personality reflect the real me. Thus, contradictions within one's self-portrait usher in doubt as to which attributes are authentic and which are phony. As one 15-year old girl put it, "I think of myself as a happy person and that feels like my true self, but then I get depressed with my parents because that isn't who I want to be, but is that my false self? Which is really me? I mean, how can I be both?" Another adolescent agonized about how, "I hate the fact that I get so nervous on a date, so inhibited. The real me is talkative [that's my natural self], but then maybe my nervous self is the real me. Am I an extravert or an introvert, I don't really know who I am." Yet another adolescent became very distraught over which of her attributes were true or phony. For example, she described how she was responsible, as well as irresponsible, smart in school, but also an "airhead" around boys. Her inability to resolve this dilemma led her to conclude, in exasperation, that, "There are days when I wish I could just become immune to myself!"

Research findings (Harter et al., 1997) reveal that concern and confusion over which of one's characteristics are one's true or false self are accompanied by a variety of distressing negative emotions. Some adolescents become anxious and agitated while others become frustrated and discouraged. Still others become depressed. From the standpoint of the *Touchstone Skills* explored in this book, it is natural, after emotions are acknowledged, for adolescents to first actively question just which of their multiple selves are authentic and which are phony. This can lead to reflecting, often with best friends with whom one shares this confusion, as they search for some clarification or confirmation of who they really are.

Fortunately, new cognitive skills emerge in later adolescence, skills that help them to reframe this issue. Two processes come to the rescue for older adolescents. First, they move to a new stage of cognitive development that supports abstract, integrative thinking. Thus, they can now combine previous developmentally lower-level contradictory concepts of self, such as cheerful versus depressed, into higher-order abstractions of being "moody" or "flexible." This advance in cognitive skill helps neutralize the conflict of multiple selves by providing a new integrative cognitive system that helps the adolescent make room for the previous contradictions, thereby diminishing concern over which characteristics are true versus which are phony.

Secondly, older adolescents develop the ability to normalize what were previously conflicting attributes. As one adolescent male put it, "It wouldn't be normal to be the same with your mother as you are with a date." Another put it this way, "You just act differently in the classroom compared to when you are at a football game with your friends; it would be weird to be the same!" Thus, this second normalization process also serves to reduce the preoccupation over which of one's characteristics is true versus false. However, concern for this dimension of one's personality does not totally abate, in part because our society does not allow for it to fade from consideration. As one develops and matures, facing a period of feeling phony may be a normative process to discovering one's authentic self.

From a broader cultural perspective, the preoccupation with authenticity can be observed in the vast vocabulary that we have developed to describe its antithesis, namely deceit, as Lerner (1993) cogently pointed out in her book entitled the *Dance of Deception.* Verb forms make reference to fabricating, withholding, concealing, distorting, falsifying, pulling the wool over one's eyes, posturing, charading, faking, and hiding behind a façade. Adjectives include evasive, elusive, wily, phony, fake, artificial, two-faced, hypocritical, manipulative, calculating, pretentious, crafty, conniving, duplicitous, deceitful, and dishonest. Noun forms include charlatan, chameleon, imposter, hypocrite, fake, and fraud. Sadly, we have far fewer words in our vocabulary to express the presence of authenticity or true self behavior. Granted, there are terms like genuine, honest, sincere, being oneself, acting in accordance with one's true self principles, being authentic, but the list is far shorter. It demonstrates an alarming focus on understanding what is inauthentic rather than on what can promote authentic behavior.

Barriers to Authenticity

Distorted perceptions of one's thoughts and emotions are harmful when they lead to faulty conclusions that prompt bad decision making. Leary (2004) observes that an egocentric approach to processing information can blind us to our shortcomings and undermine relationships with others. Self-distortion can also contribute to the misunderstanding and mismanagement of the struggles that confront us in our daily lives (Harter, 2012). Clearly, this will be an impediment in identifying authentic thoughts and feelings as well as promoting a genuine awareness of the issues and interests of the self and of others. Leary (2004) also concludes that the distortion or falsification of the self, in the form of an overestimation of one's positive qualities coupled with a preoccupation with such attributes, absorbs people in a " . . . cacophony of irrelevant self-generated thoughts" (p. 32). Such a process leaves little cognitive room for other mental processes, including attention to, and a realistic awareness of, others.

There is a need for a common language, wherein people living or working with one another and dealing with life's challenges can invoke a climate for authentic communication. We contend that the general principles of the *InAccord* model, as well as the practice of the *Touchstone Skills* of questioning, reflecting, and reframing, can provide more positive language as it helps you facilitate authenticity and encourage exploration of wording to express this authentic nature.

Quieting the Noisy Ego

Authenticity also applies to communication skills where listening to the words and opinions of others is a key component. Often one thinks about "communication" as getting one's own point of view across, forcefully asserting one's convictions and opinions. Yet equally, if not more important, is the skill of listening to what the other has to say, thereby allowing the person to tell his or her own truth. We face particular challenges in many Western societies such as the United States where, in many instances, cultural norms encourage us to speak louder and longer than the other in order to aggressively communicate our point of view. As thoughtful scholars have pointed out, the Western ego is "quite noisy" and self-aggrandizing, requiring a self-serving megaphone aimed at audiences who are hoped to be attentive and approving (Wayment & Bauer, 2008). These tendencies do not serve the goal of authentic listening. In fact, they often backfire. Thus, we need to utilize solutions for turning down the volume of the noisy ego.

In arguing for a more "quiet ego," Wayment and Bauer (2008) suggest four defining features that dovetail with the *footstep processes* and can contribute to improved communication, greater self-awareness, and expanded perspective-taking, all of which are key to authenticity. These features include: (1) *Detached awareness,* in which the person's awareness of self and other is non-defensively detached from egotistical appraisals; (2) *Interdependence,* which allows one to caringly understand others' perspectives without merely conforming to their point of view and, in doing so, maintaining one's own perspective; (3) *Compassion,* which includes empathy, acceptance, and a genuine desire to foster the well-being of others; and (4) *Growth,* which allows space and opportunity for the future positive development of both the self and others.

These concepts reinforce the necessity of applying the *footstep processes* and the *Touchstone Skills,* at the intra-psychic and interpersonal levels, in service of quieting the noisy ego. Detached awareness would seem to require the practice of all three *Touchstone Skills.* In the first instance, you first need to question your own thinking on an intra-psychic level. Secondly, detachment involves your practice of intra-psychic perspective-taking and interpersonal reflection of the other person's perspective, demonstrating a non-defensive understanding of the other's point of view. This helps prevent you from imposing your own egotistical appraisals. Finally, reframing to elicit positive meaning from the situation completes the cycle thereby allowing a new pathway to quieting the noisy ego. Interdependence builds upon reflecting skills in that it allows for mirroring differences of opinion, which can be expressed through understanding and potentially be reconciled. The practice of the

Touchstone Skills, combined with an emphasis on authenticity, also relates to the importance of transparency in that reflection encompasses empathy and acceptance for the other as his or her perspective is better understood. Wayment and Bauer's (2008) fourth defining principle, growth that promotes future positive development of both the self and the other, is facilitated by the skill of reframing. The reframing of issues into a more positive meaning promotes joint solutions and greater space in terms of creating more latitude for decision making and more opportunities for further problem solving.

Mindfulness and Authenticity

We initiated our discussion of the first footsteps of revealing emotions and empowerment by discussing mindfulness as a practice that supports each footstep. Quieting the noisy ego necessitates a return to the discussion of this essential practice and how it relates directly to the cultivation of greater authenticity. As we stated earlier, mindfulness involves a thoughtful awareness of *who one is* and *where one is* in the moment. Langer (2009) describes mindfulness as a flexible state of mind that sensitizes us to our context in the present and opens us up to novel ways of thinking. It is to be aware and attentive in the here and now; this is the essence of being "mindful." According to Thich Nhat Hahn (2013), mindfulness can be attained by moving away from dualistic thinking, such as suffering and happiness or peace and war, and moving towards a reverence for life, true happiness, true love, loving speech, deep listening, nourishment, and healing (Shambala Sun, pp. 44-48)

How does this ancient practice relate to authenticity? Mindfulness encourages us to drop the elaborate fabrication that represents an embellished storyline of our life. Too often we create an epic story akin to James Cameron's rendition of the Titanic drama where we become the tragic hero or heroine, managing to begin and end a star-crossed love affair in the time it takes the ship to sink. It may make for great theater but not for the everyday routine moments of our lives. Instead, these dramatic stories serve as modern mythology to guide us in what Joseph Campbell (1991) refers to as "The Hero's Journey." In this sense, the heroic deeds of these larger-than-life figures serve as teaching stories to entertainingly illustrate how to live an authentic life and to learn, as Campbell notes, "to follow your bliss."

But how is such mindfulness achieved? One common answer is through meditation. In meditation, one is encouraged to suspend these misguided thoughts, typically by focusing on one's breath or a simple mantra that precludes unproductive rumination. One goal of meditation is to promote mindfulness by reducing our constant mental chatter. We typically engage in considerable cluttered thinking that is reflected in our self-absorbed internal monologues as well as dialogues among our multiple selves. For example, agonizing over which of our contradictory multiple selves is our true self does not serve our search for authenticity. Such chatter diverts our attention from a more mindful focus on the present.

The *Touchstone Skills* offer another mindfulness practice that can help you quiet your noisy ego, especially when it is applied intra-psychically to expose mental chatter that may be counter-productive to your goals. When employed on a regular basis, the very act of paying attention to your habitual thinking focuses your mind into an observing self that witnesses your self-talk. The application of questioning and reflecting allows you time to bring the habitual thoughts and behaviors into greater awareness so you can evaluate their accuracy in the moment. Once exposed, your noisy ego will be less likely to drive you into reactive, predictable responses based either on an unchangeable past or on an unpredictable future. The final step of reframing the ego's self-defeating or combative talk allows you to liberate from old ways of acting and to become more authentic.

Humility

The development of humility is yet another method of quieting the noisy and self-aggrandizing ego in order to promote greater authenticity. The *Touchstone Skills* serve as a pathway to greater humility through interpersonal communication that increases your ability to understand and accept different perspectives. As Bauer and Wayment (2008) suggest, "humility can open one's mind, thus creating self-awareness that is tempered by self-compassion." In her thoughtful treatment of humility, Tangney (2009) highlights one feature that directly relates to quieting the noisy ego in order to foster authenticity. She describes humility as a "forgetting of the self," which is not the same as a "denial of the self." Rather, it requires the recognition that you are but a part of the larger universe, putting the self into perspective as a small cog in a much larger world wheel. That said, Tangney is quick to assert that humility is not self-deprecation. Rather, it involves the realistic acceptance of your limitations, as well as strengths; it realizes that you have a certain degree of personal power and self-efficacy and that you are not omnipotent. Exline (2008) concurs, suggesting that this acceptance represents a non-defensive willingness to evaluate the self accurately.

Humility requires a certain relinquishment of self-focus or self-preoccupation, which is aided by the interpersonal use of the *Touchstone Skills* to help you focus on the needs and wants of the other. As Tangney (2009) explains, "A person who has gained a sense of humility is no longer phenomenologically at the center of his or her world" (p. 484). Rather, there is a focus on the larger community of which one is a part. She develops the argument, observing that in relinquishing an egocentric focus, the person with humility becomes more open to recognizing the ability and potential worth of others, not just the self. Becoming "unselved" is Tangney's term, which is analogous to the quiet ego. A positive consequence is that you no longer need to pronounce, defend, and enhance the all-important self by negatively devaluing others. This stance of no longer finding it necessary to project your shortcomings onto another, in turn, opens you to the pathway and *footstep processes* by moving faulty perception into knowledge and creating a sense of unity verses separateness.

Dispositional Authenticity

The general principles of the *InAccord* model focus on self-awareness, empowerment, transparency, perspective-taking (spatially, emotionally and cognitively), openness to the feelings of both the self and others, which are all dimensions of authenticity. These are also echoed in Goldman's and Kernis' (2002) concept of dispositional authenticity. They identify four components: (1) self-awareness, in the form or self-understanding; (2) unbiased or realistic self-appraisals; (3) congruence between one's values, beliefs, needs, and actions; and (4) a relational orientation of being open, honest, and genuine in close relationships. Dispositional authenticity is positively correlated with greater life satisfaction and positive affect, and negatively associated with depression; that is, the more authentic the individual, the less he or she is depressed (Harter, 1999).

How do the footsteps along the pathway relate specifically to these dimensions of dispositional authenticity? Self-awareness requires transparency to be realistically in touch with one's own feelings and perspectives, as well as those of the other. Unbiased or realistic self-appraisals also stem from transparency. Congruence, from the perspective of the pathway, not only involves an integration of values, beliefs, needs, and actions, but also an appreciation for the emotions that people bring to an interpersonal problem-solving situation. These principles must be enacted with a relational orientation of mutuality in which the motives and needs of individuals are fulfilled along many dimensions (Harter, 1999).

Authenticity and the Practice of the Touchstone Skills

The goal of the *Touchstone Skills* is to help you discover rewarding solutions to both the everyday dilemmas you face as well as more acute conflicts. Questioning involves fact finding, laying the ground work, and obtaining some initial answers that bear upon the particular problematic issues which participants are confronting. Fruitful questioning is authentic and targeted at the root of the dilemma. As Leary (2004) observes, people make better life decisions if they clearly take into account accurate information about themselves that is untainted by self-serving illusions, that is, if their perceptions are realistic and authentic. Others concur, for example, Goldman (2006) links authenticity to a greater sense of self-clarity about who one is as a person. Thus, questioning needs to be approached within the context of authenticity.

The *Touchstone Skill* of reflecting moves you to a deeper level, invoking the general principles of listening with the understanding and acceptance of another. What is heard by the listener is actively reflected back to the speaker. This skill also requires authenticity that demands a clear understanding of the self. In describing "shallow thoughts about the self," Gilovich, Epley, and Hanko (2005) observe how people who are overly optimistic, overestimating their own abilities, engage in little genuine self-reflection. Rather, they engage in snap judgments that arise automatically, leading to very favorable evaluations of self, stemming from illusions of personal self-worth. Such evaluations do not originate in a reflective consideration of their true characteristics, nor do they allow the listener to reflect the speaker's perspective through a sharing of understanding in the service of mutuality (Harter, 1999).

Reframing, which involves the synthesis of the two former *Touchstone Skills*, requires the integration of authenticity as identified in the previous discussion. The task of reframing is to ask oneself and others to suspend personal judgments, such as one's own or those of the other parties, and work together to see the issue from a different angle. To think about the issue in contention differently, one must adopt a different perspective in a positive manner to move decisions forward. This is the ultimate skill that will produce progress, mutual understanding, and a solution that can be gratifying to both parties. It might involve compromise that culminates the process and is ultimately rewarding, if it can be conducted within an authentic atmosphere on the part of both parties.

We will continue to address each of these principles and the application of the *Touchstone Skills* within a variety of contexts. However, the overarching framework of authenticity, as has been demonstrated, is central to authentic communication whether it is applied to conflict resolution or to solutions to everyday challenges when people invariably must make pressing life decisions. Our respective truths may not always be in synchrony, but without expressing them, we will not be able to resolve problems in the form of acceptable solutions that will allow us to move forward.

Case Scenario: Creating an Authentic Dialogue

Now, let us explore the use of the *Touchstone Skills* in a workplace situation involving a manager and employee. Karen is a twenty-year veteran employee of the Mountain West ambulance service, working as a paramedic driving an ambulance. She is a hard worker who has passed up many opportunities over the years for advancement because she did not want to uproot her children from their home and school district. Several months ago, a new job was posted for a supervisory position and, now that her kids are grown, she quickly put in her application. However, rumors began to circulate that the job description was specifically written for a male co-worker of Karen's and that he was a shoe-in for the job. Karen refused to believe the department would choose this younger and less experienced man over her and decided to take her concerns to her direct supervisor, Terrell.

Karen's intra-psychic questioning and reflecting. Karen chose some quiet time in the evening to take out her journal and begin the process of self-inquiry. Her first step was to review her emotional feelings to find out where she was in terms of the work situation. She was a bit dismayed to find that her feelings of blame, anger, and discouragement with regard to the job opening were so strong. She knew well that these were powerful emotions that should not be taken into a workplace meeting, so she focused her self-inquiry on decreasing these emotions and increasing more positive empowering feelings like hope and happiness.

Her first question to herself had to do with her emotions as reported on the My Feelings survey, "What or who is the focus of my feelings of anger in this situation?" Her immediate response was that Terrell was often favoring male employees and so he probably was thinking of recommending a male co-worker over her. Next she began some initial reflecting. She reflected back to herself, "So, I feel that Terrell is to blame, if I do not get this new job? Is he the only person I blame?" She responded by telling herself that she blamed in anger her ex-husband for running off all those years ago and not helping raise their children or providing enough money. She reflected back, "Sounds like my ex-husband is to blame as well for not helping me with the kids." Karen knew from earlier intra-psychic questioning that this all reminded her of her childhood where her parents showered her brothers with attention and opportunities while regarding her as "just the girl." She knew this dynamic influenced a lot of her relationships with men and she did not want it to hurt her chances in the workplace. She then asked what was most upsetting about the upcoming meeting and wrote for a while about her fears and expectations. She summarized these by stating, "I am afraid to meet with Terrell because I might blow up and say something that will get me fired. Or, I might break down and cry in weakness. Either way, I do not feel there is a positive outcome in the works."

Karen's intra-psychic reframing. Karen decided to create three reframes, which served as perspective-shifting ideas, based on her journal writing of questioning and reflecting. She created the following reframe to assuage the feelings of blame. "It sounds like I am planning to blame Terrell if I do not get the job. I also know that this scenario brings up all those old hurts from childhood and from my ex-husband's abandonment. But, I know that Terrell is not my dad or my ex-husband and it is in my best interest to approach him with transparency and authenticity." She then summarized her anger over the rumors she had been hearing, trying to remove the negative. "These rumors of me being passed over for this job really have me somewhat angry and disappointed. It has been difficult to stay quiet while others talk about a young male co-worker getting the job. I even feel ready to quit if the meeting with Terrell does not go well. I also know that rumors are just that and often do not represent the truth of a situation." Her final reframing shift led her to feel reasonably confident about the upcoming meeting. "Having a meeting with Terrell is scary but I have tools to keep myself calm during the meeting and to prepare myself beforehand. In the meeting, I can use reflecting and reframing to find the positive joint solution in the conversation without letting my negative emotions jeopardize my future at the company. If I get upset, I can always ask for a time out to cool down. And, remember, I have no idea what the actual situation is with regard to the job opening."

Intra-psychic questioning revisited. Karen decided to run through one more self-talk exercise in order to prepare for her meeting the following week. She called this the "What do I really want." exercise and it consists of repeatedly asking herself, "What do I want ...really?" until she is satisfied that she has reached a core value or belief. She began this questioning and came up with the following list of deepening replies. "I want to get this job." "I want to be treated fairly." "I want to keep my job." "I want to be in the moment and not influenced by the past." "I want to be sure to make the best choice for myself." "I want to trust that I will be given what is best for me." "I want to be able to trust this process." "I want to be able to forgive if things are not done fairly." "I want peace and serenity." When she reached her ultimate goals, Karen knew that this would allow her to be more relaxed and open in the meeting with Terrell.

Terrell's intra-psychic self-talk about questioning, reflecting, and reframing. Terrell was a confident guy in his position as supervisor, and felt that he communicated well with his employees. Nevertheless, he wanted to appreciate Karen's interest in pursuing the *Touchstone Skills* that would enhance their communication. As she explained to him, this involved each of them engaging in individual self-talk about the issues that they each wanted to bring to the table. She had said it might be helpful for them each to think about the questions they had about the situation, and reflect, within themselves, about the responses to their questions, and come prepared as to how they each might reframe the situation. She had done a great deal of thinking about these issues, her emotions and interests and what might be potential solutions or outcomes. So, she encouraged him to do the same, before they met.

121

Terrell thought about this proposition. Although this was not his style, he tried to entertain the thought that this might be valuable. So what questions had he thought about? Well, he questioned "Where is Karen getting her information about a plan to hire a younger male employee for the manager's position?" He had questions about her loyalty and resolve to step into this new position. So that seemed like a good beginning point. He could reflect on why these were important questions. "Do I have doubts about Karen?' "Can I trust her?" "Am I being too harsh in my judgment of her?" "Can Karen help me understand why, in the past, she had not wanted to move up the ladder to more challenging managerial positions because she was a single mother, trying to raise three children?" "Perhaps I should be more understanding of her situation." "So how might we together reframe the situation? She was not yet aware that I was leaving, perhaps that was unfair of me to not divulge that information. Maybe I could introduce the idea of her moving with me to the new position in Arizona and explore that possibility, now that her children are grown and out on their own. It would be nice to have a loyal company member to help set up the new situation, someone who knows the ropes. So I will consider talking to her about this at their joint meeting."

Interpersonal questioning. Terrell's self-talk led him to value the importance of effective communication so when Karen suggested a format of questioning, reflecting and reframing he agreed. The meeting with Terrell was scheduled on Wednesday in the conference room where Terrell first asked Karen: "What do you need me to know most of all with regard to this situation?" Karen calmly replied, "I feel that I am the best candidate and have years more experience than my co-worker. I also heard that the job description was being rewritten to ensure that he will be a more likely candidate. When I first heard about this I was initially angry, as anyone might be, so can I please have some clarification?" Terrell then asked Karen why she wanted this job and she spent some time explaining her new freedom to take a managerial position and was even willing to move if the job dictated that. Terrell then asked Karen what specific questions she had for him. Karen asked Terrell who wrote the job description and how the decision process was structured. Terrell responded, "I wrote the job description because this position is the one I currently perform now and I know best what qualities a candidate must have. I resent the implication that I am trying to somehow 'cheat' the system by writing the description for one particular person." Karen then asked him, "I don't see any managerial positions in this regional company that are held by women. Why is that?" Terrell answered, "Actually there is one manager in Boulder who is a woman. Again, I don't like the implication that we are stacking the deck against you and other women."

Interpersonal reflecting. Terrell reflected back Karen's original statement by saying, "You feel that you are the best candidate for this job and have many more years experience than the person in question. You also heard a rumor that this job was written for a younger male colleague this person and that made you somewhat angry." He then summarized her second response by noting, "It sounds like you are ready to advance in the company and have the freedom to move if that is in the job description. It may also be that you are pretty burned out and need a break from direct ambulance work." Karen then reflected back Terrell's comments, "Thank you, you are right. I am pretty burned out. I hear you saying that you wrote this job description because the person will be performing the skills you do right now in your job. You resent the implication that you are somehow cheating the system by writing the job for a particular person." Terrell nodded his head in agreement. Karen continued, "It also sounds like there is one manager in this region who is a woman and you also resent the implication that the deck is stacked against women like me advancing at work."

At this point Terrell suggested they continue the questioning and reflecting a bit longer in order to build a stronger connection so they could problem solve together. Karen started by restating her feelings and adding, "My current job is intensely stressful and I feel like all these years of dealing with emergency after emergency is unrewarded. At times I feel somewhat angry and unappreciated." Terrell reflected back, "Karen I hear that you have worked for 20 years at a high level of stress and believe you have the experience to do this new job. You feel that you are not sufficiently appreciated and have some legitimate anger about this." Terrell reflected back, "I should have realized you were angry and felt unappreciated." At this point, Karen visibly relaxed and nodded her head. Next, Terrell provided more information, "Karen, you have put your name in for a management position in the past and then not taken the job. This makes me question your loyalty to the company. It makes me angry that you are taking the rumors as fact and that you did not give me the benefit of the doubt in this situation." Karen reflected back, "Terrell, it sounds like you are impacted by my applying for this position in the past and then withdrawing my application. You are also angry because I assumed the rumors were true instead of checking them out right away."

Karen then remarked, "I passed up other opportunities because I was a single parent raising three kids. Two of the manager openings would have meant me either working nights or moving to another city. I had to put my kids' needs first and so I stayed as a paramedic much longer than I ever intended. To me, was never about loyalty or I would have gone to work somewhere else." Terrell reflected, "You passed up many opportunities for advancement to take care of your children. It was not about loyalty but about putting your kids first." Terrell then remarked, "Karen, I want you to know that I did not write the job description for any one person. I wrote this because I need someone with excellent communication skills, a good work ethic, and a commitment and loyalty to the company. There are four applicants in final consideration for this job and you all have met or exceeded the criteria in at least two of these areas. As of today, I have not made up my mind and will not do so for at least another 30 days." Karen reflected, "It sounds like you have a group of four employees under consideration for this job and that you did not write the description for any one person. Your goal is to find a person with good communication skills, a good work ethic, and loyalty and commitment to the company."

Interpersonal reframing. Terrell and Karen used the process of reflecting for the first half hour of the meeting and then decided to move to reframing in order to find joint solutions so that they could move forward. Terrell began, "It sounds like you need to know how I will make this decision so you can be satisfied that it was made fairly." Karen agreed that she needed more transparency with the process and shared her shift in perspective in the following statement, "I understand that this is not a decision that is easy for you because three people are bound to be upset or disappointed at the end of the process. I also understand that you believe I have an excellent work ethic and very good communication skills at work.

Terrell shifted his perspective and reframed the dilemma into a problem solving solution. "Karen, I cannot promise you that you will have the job even though you have affirmed your commitment and loyalty; however, I will say that it does improve your chances of getting the job. What I will work hard to do is to have this selection process be as transparent as possible. To that end, I will arrange similar meetings with the other three applicants this week and then one final meeting with each of you within thirty days. After that, I will make my decision and let each of you know my rationale."

Terrell recommended to the owners of the company that they consider the process he was using with the four finalists across the entire workforce for any new hire or promotion. Karen noted that she thought this process would help not only with the natural disappointment of not getting a promotion but would improve overall job performance for any applicant. Karen reflected on her emotions and noted that she had a marked decrease in the intensity of disempowering emotions concerning this situation and greater increase in the intensity of the empowering emotions. She knew that, although it will be disappointing if she does not get the job, she will be accepting of the decision.

Epilogue. When Karen found out about the decision, she was neither angry nor discouraged but chose to believe that she would be first in line for the next opening that was slated for the end of the year. Karen's greater acceptance of a decision that did not favor her is based on the willingness of Terrell to join with Karen in a communication process based on transparency and authenticity. Terrell did have information that he was not permitted to share during his meetings with Karen. The company was opening a new regional office in Arizona and he had been offered the directorship of the entire operation. He wanted to be sure to leave someone in charge of his former position who could seamlessly take over his tasks without direction. Thus he appointed the young man whom he felt could handle the position.

Terrell planned to offer Karen a supervisory position in the new region. During the meeting, Terrell was impressed at their ability to communicate, using the *Touchstone Skills*. If Karen had never asked for the meeting or if she had kept silent, she would have missed out on this opportunity because Terrell assumed she was still unable to move out of the area. In the end, Karen accepted a position to move to the Arizona office. Her reframe involved her looking forward to moving to a new, warmer part of the country. She was tired of driving an ambulance in the snows of Colorado, a harrowing part of the job. Plus, her grown children would look forward to visiting her in Arizona. It is closer to where they now live. Her reframe involved an appreciation and flexibility to meet the needs of both herself and Terrell.

Survey on Authentic Communication

A central theme of this book is the role of authenticity in people's relationships. Authenticity may be valued and enacted by some, whereas for others, it may represent a challenge and may be viewed as having a downside in relationships. The purpose of the following survey is to help you think about your own personal views on authenticity.

Simply check one of the four response options for each statement that is most true for you. There are only ten items. These items reflect a range of attitudes. There are neither right nor wrong answers and this is most certainly not a test. The survey was designed merely to alert you as to how some of these issues may play out in your own thinking about relationships. This survey is entirely confidential and you do not need to reveal your responses to anyone else.

If you choose to do so, you may sum your scores to the ten items (the possible scores are 4, 3, 2, or 1 and are given in parentheses after each response choice (Really True, Sort of True, etc.). Note that some items are scored 1, 2, 3, 4, given how items are worded; this is a common feature of good surveys. After you calculate this sum of your ten scores, divide the sum by 10. This will give you your overall, average score. Higher scores indicate that you value authenticity and try to practice it in your relationships. Lower scores indicate that you legitimately question the value of authenticity because it might threaten relationships or that you find it challenging or difficult to engage in authenticity.

Please review each statement below and choose **ONLY ONE RESPONSE FROM THE FOUR**. If you feel that two responses might apply, please decide on which one *is TRUER for you*. Do not check in between the words or statements.

1. Although it is a challenge figuring out how to express my true feelings in a relationship, in the long run it is worth it.

☐ Very true (4) ☐ Sort of true (3) ☐ Not very true (2) ☐ Not at ALL true (1)

2. I sometimes find it hard to be my true self in personal relationships.

☐ Very true (1) ☐ Sort of true (2) ☐ Not very true (3) ☐ Not at ALL true (4)

3. I think it is important to say, in a caring way, what I really feel in a close relationship. I try my best to do so.

☐ Very true (4) ☐ Sort of true (3) ☐ Not very true (2) ☐ Not at ALL true (1)

4. While it is easier, sometimes, to *not* express my true feelings in a relationship, ultimately that feels phony to me and can end up backfiring, so I try to express them.

☐ Very true (4) ☐ Sort of true (3) ☐ Not very true (2) ☐ Not at ALL true (1)

5. It is a challenge for me to say what I really think in a close relationship, sometimes it is just easier not to express what I really think or feel.

☐ Very true (1) ☐ Sort of true (2) ☐ Not very true (3) ☐ Not at ALL true (4)

6. I try not to "rock the boat" by telling someone what I really think or feel, in order to preserve the relationship.

☐ Very true (1) ☐ Sort of true (2) ☐ Not very true (3) ☐ Not at ALL true (4)

7. Being authentic in a relationship is a goal for me and, therefore, I try to constructively express my true thoughts and feelings.

☐ Very true (4) ☐ Sort of true (3) ☐ Not very true (2) ☐ Not at ALL true (1)

8. It's often difficult to express what I am really thinking in an authentic manner that is constructive.

☐ Very true (1) ☐ Sort of true (2) ☐ Not very true (3) ☐ Not at ALL true (4)

9. I sometimes find it easier to avoid expressing differences of opinion in a close relationship. In the short run, it can compromise my true self, but I still prefer not to express differences of opinion.

☐ Very true (1) ☐ Sort of true (2) ☐ Not very true (3) ☐ Not at ALL true (4)

10. Honesty may not be the best policy. Being too honest can harm a close relationship so I tend to avoid it.

☐ Very true (1) ☐ Sort of true (2) ☐ Not very true (3) ☐ Not at ALL true (4)

SUM OF TEN ITEM SCORES = _____ Divide this score by 10 to achieve your overall average score of _____ which should be between 4 and 1.

Summary of your Movement along the Pathway

In the preceding chapters, you have been introduced to the *Touchstone Skills* as well as the *footstep processes.* We have demonstrated how mastery of these skills and processes can help your journey along the pathway toward change that will help to resolve a dilemma. You have completed surveys that allow you to assess where you stand on the various *Touchstone Skills* and the *footstep processes* along the pathway. You may have your own personal views about how to move your own life along the pathway and what you need to do in order to enact these principles in your own life.

To aid in this thought process, we present a Table below that first respects the fact that people will have different styles in addressing the footsteps along the pathway. We have compressed the survey content into two general styles, one in the first column on the left and another in the second column on the right. Take one topic at a time, listed in the middle of the column, and decide whether your style is more like the one described in the left column or whether your style is more like the more portrayed in the right column. Give this some thought. This is an opportunity for you to gather your thoughts and knowledge about these concepts, and honestly reflect on your own style.

What we have included in this table, in each box, is a description **in bold print** of a given style, so you can identify your own. Below each style description are suggestions for what you might do to move forward along the pathway. This will differ, depending on your style. We hope these will be helpful as you continue on your journey toward resolution and self-liberation.

Table 2. Differing Styles of Communication along the Pathway

RECOGNIZING COMMUNICATION CHALLENGES	RECOGNIZING COMMUNICATION STRENGTHS
Revealing Emotions	
I do not seem to be in touch with my emotions or feelings so it is difficult to communicate them to another. If you have trouble revealing your emotions, begin with Touchstone Practice of *intra-psychic* questioning of your true feelings.	**I can pretty readily reveal my emotions and feelings but need to work on how to communicate them to others.** If you are in this camp, your Touchstone Practice begins with sharing with close friends how you *feel* versus what you are *thinking*.
Empowerment	
I think empowerment is prideful and aggressive and I would rather be liked than feared. An empowered person does not act aggressively in order to intimidate others, it is not power over but power within. This inner power creates a strength that will help you when you need the courage to face a dilemma or resolve a situation.	**I feel that increasing personal empowerment is a good thing for me; however, I don't see how practicing the intra-psychic and interpersonal skills would lead me to feel more empowered.** Every skill that you practice with yourself and with others improves your overall communication skills, which leads to greater confidence the next time you face a dilemma.

Gaining Perspective	
I find it hard to take another person's perspective because I usually think mine is more accurate and don't particularly want to change it if we do not agree.	**Seeing things from another person's point of view can improve communication within a relationship. But, I sometimes have trouble doing this when there is a difference of opinion.**
Think of this as an investment in your relationships. These skills are designed to help you reflect on the question *"What do I want, really? What do those I am relationship with want, really"*	Think about this as a pathway to your true self. We can share with you our ideas and concepts but what is meaningful is to directly experience the power of the Touchstones by implementing them in all your relations.
Empathy and Compassion	
This is a pretty tall order, when so many people focus on themselves. I have to look out for myself. I could get hurt by attempting to be empathic or compassionate.	**These seem like basic human values that would improve a relationship, fostering its further growth. But it seems as if both parties have to agree and work together on these skills and I wonder how that can be fostered.**
Being empathic and having compassion *is* watching out for you. These qualities serve not only for understanding the other, but being understood yourself.	Empathy and Compassion become natural processes and a way of being. When you model this, you may find that others around you naturally tend to embrace the qualities for themselves.

Transparency	
To enact these communication skills you have to be very open about your thoughts and feelings, something that I am not comfortable doing. I am not certain that it will improve my relationships. The rewards of being transparent, *meaning what you think, say, feel and do are aligned,* allow for a steady stance as you face day to day situations. You can now share who you are in good and bad times and transition much more quickly from a difficult situation to a more balanced life.	**I like the idea of being open and honest about my thoughts and feelings in a relationship, but need some advice about just how to do so.** By integrating the Touchstones of questioning, reflecting and reframing, you create a communication practice that is so attractive, others will want to be in your company. This begets deeper and stronger personal connections.
Authenticity	
I have difficulty expressing my true self in interpersonal relationships, it seems better not to reveal too much. Discernment may be appropriate. Put as much effort into *understanding the other* and you may then feel at ease to open up your true self to others.	**I feel I can express my true self and viewpoints openly, but sometimes not in the most caring or constructive manner.** Demanding someone see *your perspective* may damage the relationship. It may be prudent to *reflect* through your self- talk on how another might receive your feedback.

Resolution/Self-Liberation	
I realize that I need to become more aware of all of these processes. I am just not certain that I can meet all of these objectives in order to achieve self-liberation, it seems too overwhelming. Learning these skills and applying them across your life is a direction, not a goal. It is good to think about taking it one day at a time so you do not become overwhelmed.	**I can see how integrating these skills will help me become a better communicator and achieve self-liberation. What about the times I fail to communicate skillfully?** It can help to remember that this is a pathway circle that you will travel many times. Each time you use these skills and processes they become more integrated and habitual. Mistakes are a necessary part of the learning process and only indicate you need to get back on pathway.

Chapter Six
Using the Touchstone Skills to Bridge Cultural Divides

Human behavior is greatly influenced by underlying beliefs, values, and assumptions. These beliefs, values, and assumptions are, largely, a by-product of culture. Ting-Toomey and Chung (2005) define culture as a learned meaning system that consists of patterns of traditions, beliefs, values, norms, meanings, and symbols that are passed on from one generation to the next and are shared to varying degrees by interacting members of a community. Most of the time we are not conscious of how culture influences our values, beliefs, assumptions and our behaviors because culture is so all-encompassing. (see Ries & Harter, 2012)

Overview

In this chapter, we will demonstrate how the *footstep processes* help create a communication template that can also serve as a safe arena for difficult conversations based on cultural, religious, or ethnic differences. Cultural differences and misperceptions can inadvertently compromise communication when two people have not agreed upon speaking in a manner that promotes authenticity and ensures civility. This chapter demonstrates how the *Touchstone Skills* can provide important tools for those interested in authentic, civil discourse. We illustrate this framework by applying it to the very complex cultural problem of immigration into the United States with both a Chinese immigrant, Chen, and a Mexican immigrant, Maria. Each immigrant uses these skills to ease their transition into a new country. These case examples include the cultural models of assimilation and integration, biculturation and adaptation, and high and low context cultures, each interwoven with the *Touchstone Skills* and *footstep processes.*

Case Study: Adapting to a New Culture

There is perhaps no other cultural issue more in need of the civilizing influence of skillful communication than that of immigration. Often the very real concerns of assimilation and adaptation, economic ramifications, and extension of basic human rights are overshadowed by simplistic arguments based on the host culture's fear of differences. Immigration habitually becomes a political rallying point for opposing sides as some politicians seek to garner more power by appealing to the host culture with messages of divisiveness. The *Touchstone Skills* can serve the immigrants themselves as they embark on an extremely challenging journey that demands a high level of effective communication as well as those who are impacted by the immigrant's entry into their established community.

Immigrant dilemmas can be understood more clearly by examining various models of cultural integration that provide a larger context for their issues. Early single-continuum models of cultural integration tended to focus on only two choices, to totally retain traditional values or to reject these values and totally embrace the values of the new host country. In such a single continuum model, the culturally-ethnocentric implication was that the total assimilation of the dominant cultural values was the "healthier" psychological choice in terms of adaptation. However, more complex models have evolved (see Berry, 1980, 2005), revealing that immigrants have a more complicated set of choices and decisions to make, cultural problem-solving tasks that can be fostered constructively or actively thwarted by the host culture. Our *Touchstone Skills* and *footstep processes,* when used during the experience of immigration, may assist new bi-dimensional models to evolve. Consider Figure 2 below where an individual can be located in one of four quadrants that represent four types of adaptation.

Figure 2.

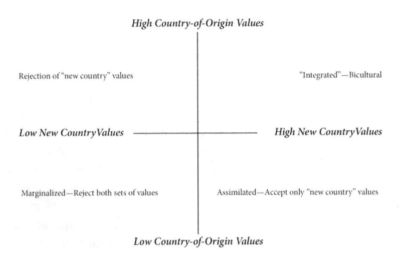

High Country-of-Origin Values

Rejection of "new country" values   "Integrated"—Bicultural

Low New Country Values ——————————— High New Country Values

Marginalized—Reject both sets of values   Assimilated—Accept only "new country" values

Low Country-of-Origin Values

Let's consider the case of Chen, an immigrant from China coming to the United States to seek an American education, work opportunities, and join other members of his family that have immigrated in the past. Chen's move requires that he develop advanced communication tools to help him make many decisions and face numerous social and psychological challenges. The *Touchstone Skills* are embedded within such communication skills and will support Chen with the many decisions and challenges which are inherent in adapting to a host country such as the United States. Moreover, the stance of the community he enters will impact Chen's adjustment in terms of the ease with which he can adapt to new cultural demands. In Chen's case, the *footstep processes* and the use of the *Touchstone Skills* can help him with many of his decisions and associated dilemmas.

Let us begin with a major challenge that faces immigrants like Chen, where they must confront two very different sets of values and beliefs, those from their culture of origin and those from the community they are entering, in this case, the city of US city of San Francisco. Chen will be faced with many decisions regarding whether or not to retain and embrace the values of his traditional culture, which might result in rejecting the dominant values of San Francisco. Alternatively, he will face the challenge of directly or inadvertently abandoning some Chinese traditions and values in order to more rapidly assimilate into the new dominant American society.

Berry (2005) defines those as high on the values of both one's culture of origin and American culture, those in the upper right quadrant, as "integrated." Chen falls into this quadrant because he has a commitment to maintain his original Chinese cultural traditions while adopting some American values and customs. In his case, he developed strong ties to the local Chinese community in his new hometown of San Francisco. At the same time, he joined an intermural softball team at his college. In this way, Chen makes an effort to retain the integrity of the values of his country of origin while at the same time seeking to behave in accordance with the values of the dominant American culture. On the pathway to self-liberation, these distinctions are identified and affirmed through the *Touchstone Skills* of questioning, reflecting, and reframing and the integration of the *footstep processes*.

The assimilation strategy is displayed by a friend of Chen's from Taiwan who chose not to maintain the values of his original culture but rather vigorously embrace the tenets of the San Francisco by displaying strong American values and traditions. His friend, and others like him from Asian countries, tends to fall into the lower right hand quadrant of High New Country values and Low Country of Origin Values. On the opposite end, we find Chen's aunt who speaks little English after 50 years in the host country. She displays the rejection of the dominant culture in San Francisco, in the upper left-hand quadrant, where individuals place a premium on maintaining their original cultural values and traditions. These individuals actively attempt to reject host country values and not assimilate the values, beliefs, or traditions of the host country. In the lower left-hand quadrant, we can find those immigrants who are "marginalized," denying an interest in either set of cultural values. In some ways, this is a no man's land where Berry (2005) observes many experience enforced cultural loss and show little desire to interact with others, often in response to exclusion or discrimination. In previous labeling schemes, this quadrant has been called "deculturalization."

Berry (2005) has made the point that the adoption of these different cultural strategies assumes that ethnic-minority individuals coming to the dominant culture have the freedom to choose how they want to acculturate; they can select the quadrant of their choice. However, he thoughtfully observes that the immigrants' success in realizing their adaptation goals will depend upon the attitudes of members in the dominant culture. For example, a desire to be in the "integrated" or bicultural quadrant, retaining the values of one's culture of origin but also embracing or endorsing American values, will only be successful if the dominant culture is open and inclusive, where cultural diversity is valued in what Berry calls an atmosphere of "multiculturalism." Thus, the dominant culture must be supportive in this endeavor. Chen's experience of settling into San Francisco with a large and growing population of Chinese immigrants and a thriving Chinese community allowed him to easily adopt a more integrated lifestyle. He also found that integrating the *Touchstone Skills* of questioning, reflecting, and reframing into his communication style was vital to his understanding and appreciation of the perspectives of the American cultural system of values and beliefs.

Chen's Use of the Touchstone Skills

Immigrants like Chen who gravitate toward the upper right quadrant of what Berry calls "integration," can more easily use the *Touchstone Skills* both at the intra-psychic level of self-talk and the interpersonal level, in dialogues between themselves and members of the dominant, host country. Although questioning, reflecting, and reframing were not forms of communication Chen learned in China, his adoption of them in the United States afforded him a deeper clarity about the similarities and differences of Chinese and American beliefs and tradition. This clarity increased his sense of empowerment, an important footstep on the pathway, as he tried on new values from America while keeping his own intact.

In the example of Chen's "empowering journey," he was discussing the actual term "empowerment" with an American friend. He remarked that there was an old Chinese proverb that states "Endure a little more, then you can avoid a stormy sea, retreat one step backwards, then you can see a clear sky." He revealed that in China, people facing adversity tended to endure and to adapt gradually (Yang, 1995). He also noted that, unlike Americans, the Chinese preferred gradual rather than radical or more immediate empowerment because gradual empowerment translated into endurance and transcendence from suffering to blessing. He and his friend engaged in a long and lively conversation about their perspectives, each appreciatively listening to the other's views. Because Chen was willing to integrate the skills along the pathway, rather than automatically adapt, he slowly found greater self-liberation that combined the American emphasis on building up the individual self and the Chinese importance of transcending suffering through love and forgiveness.

Chen came to believe he was living in the best of both worlds. Chen told a friend who was struggling with integrating his Chinese way of life with his new American reality, "There is a price to pay for citizenship in this country but it does not have to be assimilation or rejection. The price is to commit to a journey along the pathway, using the *Touchstone Skills* to uncover the mysteries of the American culture while appreciating that it can enhance, and on occasion supersede, our own strong traditions."

Chen's integration is tied directly to the perspective of an immigrant who must make critical decisions. For example, his self-talk may involve such questioning as: "Do I accurately perceive the situation?" "Can I respond in this situation and still respect both sets of cultural values?" "Do I need more information before engaging in a conversation with American acquaintances?" Consider Chen's use of the *Touchstone Skills* through his first practice with the intramural softball team at his university. At his first practice, he noted a difference between the much stronger emphasis of Chinese competition focused on team and country as opposed to the tendency for his American teammates to focus on individual accomplishment.

Chen's intra-psychic reflecting may take the following form: "Am I perceiving this difference in competition accurately or am I missing some element that can tie my traditions to my teammates?" "Who on the team is acting in more of an individual manner and who is more of a team player?" "Maybe I am generalizing too much and not taking into account those who are exhibiting more of a team spirit." Chen's intra-psychic reframing could involve such conclusions as, "I think I can figure out when it is appropriate to engage in behaviors that represent the values of my own culture and when to display American values, appropriately." " It's important for me to be clear about how to behave in different situations, for example, engaging in the values of my primary culture with family and close immigrant friends, but respecting American values when I am with Americans at work or in social situations." "In the case of my teammates, it appears that the more individualistic teammates are able to act somewhat independently and still support the team through their efforts. And, most of the players are team-focused and they seem to be more integrated into the team than the perceived "stars" of the team. This is much more in keeping with my values and I will use these players as role models more than the individualistic ones."

Interpersonal questioning. Chen came into more contact with resistance to his immigrant status at the University where some students resented his high marks on tests and ability to easily grasp engineering concepts. This became clear at a study group where Chen could feel undercurrents of animosity from a particular student, Alan. Chen decided to be more direct than was the Chinese custom while honoring his Chinese values of humility. He asked Alan directly, "Are you feeling unhappy with my participation in this group?" "Is there something in particular that you are upset about?"

Interpersonal reflecting. Alan shared that it was hard for him to keep up with Chen when he started talking about an engineering formula. He noted that it was intimidating and he did not want to appear stupid in front of the others by asking Chen questions. Chen reflected Alan's concerns exactly, which made Alan feel that Chen really wanted to understand and cared about Alan. Chen then shared with Alan that in China the education system was much more focused on the sciences than in the U.S. and he noted it put him at an advantage in America. He also stressed that his culture was also based on Confucianism, which accents communal endeavors as a path to perfection. In this sense, he always believed his work was to help the group as well as himself. Alan was relieved and surprised to find that Chen was not as competitive as his American friends and that he did not come off as superior in any way. He remarked to Chen, "Although we come from different cultures, I feel we have enough in common to respect and understand each other."

Interpersonal reframing. Reframing helped Chen focus the conversation on mutual helpfulness rather than competition. He reframed Alan's statement about feeling stupid as "I now realize that it is important to know more about how Americans express themselves. It sounds like you feel a pressure to listen to me without asking questions because you fear your friends will judge you. It also sounds like I talk fast and it might help if I slowed down a bit and allowed time for questions." Alan was delighted to find that Chen understood his dilemma and was willing to help him. Chen began to understand how some parts of American competitiveness were not only difficult for him but for Americans as well. He suggested a solution to Alan's fear of asking questions by agreeing to stop at particular points in his presentations to the group to ask directly for questions. Not surprisingly, Chen and Alan became good friends during their University years, and Alan learned as much about Chinese culture as Chen did about his newly adopted country.

High and Low Context Cultural Communication Differences

Chen was fortunate to be introduced to anthropologist Edward T. Hall's theory of the powerful effect of high and low context cultures in a class at the University. High context in this instance refers to high on collaboration and more relational approaches to communication versus low collaboration and a more directive approaches to communication. Hall (1976) refers to context as the framework, background, and surrounding circumstances in which communication or an event takes place. He noted that where high- context and low- context cultures intersect, there was often a disconnect in communication that may never be addressed. Many individuals from high-context cultures favor an indirect verbal style; prefer ambiguous, cautious, and non-confrontational ways of working through communication issues; rely on nonverbal behaviors and subtleties, and are very listener-oriented. High- context cultures tend to place a higher value on harmony, tactfulness, and saving face. Someone from a high-context culture will likely ease into a conversation and may wait to be invited to speak or request permission before talking. Individuals will first connect on a relational level and only after that has occurred, introduce substantive issues. According to Hall, these cultures are collectivist, preferring group harmony and consensus to individual achievement. Additionally, people in these cultures are less governed by reason than by intuition or feelings. Words are not so important as context, which might include the other's tone of voice, facial expression, gestures, posture—and even the person's family history and status. Immigrants from high- context cultures such as much of the Middle East, Asia, Africa, and South America, tend to have more difficult adjusting to American's low context manner of communicating (see also Harter, 2012).

Low-context cultures which include North America and Western Europe prefer communication that is direct and frank and they tend to be more logical, linear, individualistic, and action-oriented. In these cultures, an open confrontation of issues is ideal and a speaker-orientation is valued. Directness and self-assertion are preferred in low-context cultures such that individual will likely verbally assert him or herself into a conversation and will promptly acknowledge substantive issues directly.

It is important to note that one communication style is not better or worse than another, simply different. High-context immigrants who relocate to the United States can be helped greatly by understanding the different manner in which Americans converse. They can also use the *Touchstone Skills* to find out where and when communication is breaking down simply due to this cultural phenomenon. In Chen's case, he understood immediately that he needed to be more direct with his American friends and colleagues, yet it was not a natural style for him. He often used questioning and reflecting to be sure he understood his American colleagues and that they understood him.

Are Those in the High American/High Asian Quadrants Truly Integrated?

From the previous discussion, it would appear that the general principles of the *InAccord* model can be most productively applied to immigrants like Chen who desires to be in the integrated quadrant, particularly if the dominant host respects cultural diversity and welcomes him into an atmosphere of multiculturalism. Recall that Berry has labeled this quadrant, high on both sets of cultural values, "integrated", implying that somehow the individual has truly combined or transformed the values of both cultures into one amalgamated set of values that speak with a single voice.

Susan Harter, in collaboration with a Ph.D. student, Tara Mehta, who came to this country from India, challenged the notion that individuals in this quadrant were "truly integrated". Mehta, in immigrating to the United States, had her own experiences to draw upon. She and Harter suggested that those in the upper right quadrant who endorsed both sets of values at high levels might find themselves in a position where different values could comfortably co-exist but represented parallel orientations that were displayed appropriately in each separate cultural context. However, they questioned whether this orientation was truly "integrated".

Here, they were drawn to the thinking of several cross-cultural researchers who have spoken to the issues of biculturalism. Cross & Gore (2003) have summarized the literature revealing that individuals who experience more than one culture display new self-representations that come to co-exist with the self-representations from their culture of origin. When two cultural forms of self-appraisal may alternately be triggered in everyday life, individuals have been observed to engage in "cultural frame switching" (Hong, Morris, Chiu, & Benet-Marinez,

2000). The person selects behaviors appropriate for a given cultural contexts, which is precisely how Chen adapted to US values. This flexible application of cultural knowledge results in adaptive reactions to the shifting bicultural milieu.

In questioning whether the High American/High Asian quadrant represented "true integration" versus a more "bicultural adaptation", Harter and Mehta wanted to move beyond mere speculation. Thus, in a dissertation by Mehta (2005) which is reported in Harter (2012), Mehta recruited participants (students originally from India but who have lived in Chicago for at least 10 years). They were presented with a task that identified four written options, each of which was accompanied by a puzzle-like drawing that visually depicted each choice (see Figure 3 on the following page). They sought to examine four different orientations: (a) true integration, (b) unhealthy fragmentation, (c) healthy differentiation, and (d) no interest/reflection.

The first option, to measure true integration read, "How I am with different people all fits together nicely into a single me; it adds up to my sense of myself as a whole person." The second option was designed to reflect a less healthy form that implies unhealthy fragmentation, where the description was, "How I am with different people does not all fit together in one piece, and that feels uncomfortable or distressing to me." The third option, healthy differentiation, was designed to assess the comfortable coexistence of each acculturation style or strategy, "How I am with different people does not all fit together in one piece, but that feels OK to me." The fourth option, representing no interest/reflection," read, "I don't think a lot about how I am with different people or how it fits together."

Figure 3.

1. Read each statement and look at the puzzle next to it. Check the box that best describes how you really are.

☐ (A) How I am with different people all <u>fits together</u> nicely into a single me. It adds up to a sense of myself as a whole person.

☐ (B) How I am with different people doesn't all fit together in one piece, and that <u>feels uncomfortable</u> or <u>distressing</u> to me.

☐ (C) How I am with different people doesn't all fit together in one piece, but that <u>feels OK</u> to me.

☐ (D) I don't think a lot about how I am with different people or how it fits together.

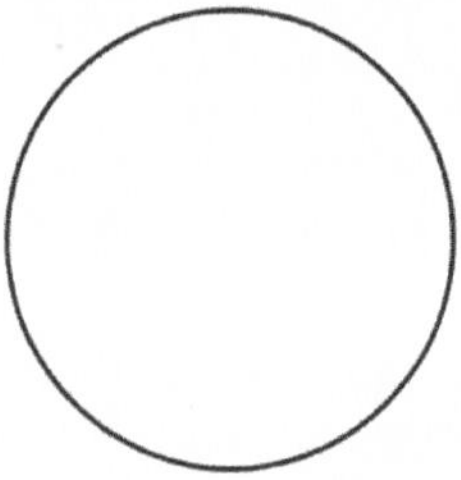

Mehta and Harter (see Harter, 2012) predicted that the majority of her sample from India would select the "healthy differentiation" option and that relatively few would endorse the "integrated" choice. These predictions were supported in that 70% did select the "healthy differentiation" choice, whereas only 13% selected the "integrated" option. Another 13% chose the "unhealthy fragmentation" option, with only 4% selecting the fourth "no interest, no reflection" choice.

Based on this pattern of findings, they suggested that the high/high quadrant should not be conceptualized as "integration" given that this label did not capture most respondents' psychological experience. Rather, "bi-cultural" appears to be a more appropriate designation, because almost three fourths of respondents indication that each set of values could appropriate co-exist. The term "integration", they feel, implies a different psychological process that is not borne out by our results. Their conclusion is consistent with the perspective of Friedman and Liu (2009) who define biculturalism as the ability to comfortably understand and act in accordance with the norms, ways of thinking, and attitudes of two cultural systems. The bicultural individual also has the ability to shift between these two value systems appropriately, as the situation demands. It is in this quadrant, high country of origin/high new country values, where they have previously argued that the *footstep processes* and the *Touchstone Skills* are most applicable, in facilitating an adaptive bi-cultural perspective.

Case Scenario: Gone to the Dogs

In 2012, first author Ries and Mediators Without Borders Instructor Brian Luther traveled to Romania to conduct a mediation and arbitration training in Constanta by the Black Sea. Against the beautiful backdrop of this seaside city, they began to notice that there were dogs running wild on the streets and beaches; lots of dogs. They noticed that patrons arriving and leaving the hotel were shaking their pant legs, trying to keep the dogs from ripping their clothes and biting them. As cars went past, packs of dogs would chase them and bite at the tires. Not surprisingly, many of these dogs had only three legs but still they chased cars and harassed pedestrians. Ries and Luther both wondered why the local citizens would let this hazardous situation continue and not round up the dogs and take them to a shelter. What they found was that the dilemma of the dogs was deeply embedded in the former communist years that stripped many Romanians of their land and rights.

When the communists seized control of Romania, many rural people were forced off their farms and into stark apartment buildings in urban areas. The Romanians reported that the communist leaders forbade these people to bring any animals with them and so the bereft owners set the animals free to fend for themselves rather than destroy them. The release of many dogs onto the streets became a symbol of a freedom that the owners no longer enjoyed. Soon the released dogs began to run in packs and harass people in the city. Many attempts were made to capture the dogs. However, when the dogs were captured, citizens who identified with their symbolic importance would adopt them and then set them free again. One man remarked to Ries that it gave him a sense of power to release them and that made up in some small measure for all he lost under the communist rule. However, she heard a restaurant owner grumbling one evening about how he would like to take all the mangy creatures out in a boat and drown them.

With each passing year since the overthrow of the communist regime, there is growing pressure from new business owners, parents who want their children to be able to play safely outside, and tourists wanting to enjoy the beach to do something about this troubling and dangerous situation. However, the emotional link to the freedom of these dogs runs very deep and is also strongly tied to feelings of empowerment. Another woman reported to Ries that she felt this sinking feeling when she watched a dog be captured because it reminded her of the time when she was forced from her home and into a bleak over-crowded apartment. It seemed as if letting the dogs run free became a symbolic statement of the resistance to anyone ever taking away the freedom of the Romanian people again. The dilemma is between two groups: (1) those who directly experienced the hopelessness of the communist takeover and had to release their dogs or knew someone who did; and (2) those citizens who did not directly experience the change in regime and whose business success relies on containment of the wild dogs.

Identifying Emotions. This is a dilemma that calls for revealing emotions among both groups. The group that wants something done about the dogs reports feeling anxiety about their personal success in their businesses and anger about the inability of their countrymen to move past the historical grief about the dogs being released on the streets. In contrast, those directly impacted by releasing their pets onto the streets, feel depression and despair as they consider the historic fate of their beloved animals.

In order to facilitate a joint solution, there needs to be a forum where people can express their emotions regarding the dogs. This could set the stage for a dialogue among the citizens to use questioning, reflecting, and reframing and build understanding to create a resolution that meets the needs of all the citizens. It is important to understand that although Romania is part of the European Union, it is not a western low- context society but representative of the eastern European high- context style. As we mentioned earlier in this chapter, people in cultures like Romania tend to be more governed by intuition or feelings than by reason; therefore, words are not so important as context, which might include the speaker's tone of voice, facial expression, gestures, posture—and even the person's family history and status. This is very important to consider when applying any communication intervention.

Taking the Two Groups through the Touchstone Skills. The first statement by the countryman who had to release his dog relayed his feeling of empowerment when he adopted a dog and then released it again onto the beach. In order to facilitate a dialogue in this case, the a business owner who would like to have the dogs contained might ask him, "Tell me more about this feeling of empowerment you are talking about." "What about the dogs being free makes you feel empowered?" In this case, he may remark, "I know these dogs are a nuisance but when I think about them sitting alone in a wire cage, I feel enraged." "When I see the dogs running free on the beach, I remember my childhood on my father's farm. I used to run through the fields and climb trees and then one day the communists came and took everything away in an instant." "But, I also see that the dogs are hungry and hurt and I just look away because I don't know what to do anymore. Truth is, I hate seeing how they suffer but I don't want them killed off either."

In this case, where emotions are running high, it would be advisable for the business oriented group to mirror back this man's historical grief as closely as possible so that he feels heard and understood. Once he begins to feel heard, the business man can start to reframe some of his statements and focus the two of them on joint solutions. He could begin with, "I hear you say that although you know the dogs are a nuisance, it is very upsetting for you to watch the dogs captured because you imagine them sitting alone in cages. It sounds like you enjoy seeing the dogs running on the beach because it reminds you of the time in your childhood when you were also running free on the farm. Then, everything changed and you could no longer have that freedom." This understanding could be followed by a reframing with a solution- focused question such as, "I also hear you say that you know something has to be done and that the dogs are often hurt or hungry. But, you don't want to see them killed either. I wonder if there is some solution between letting them run free and having them destroyed or permanently locked up."

As the individual with historical grief begins to feel more empowered by the other man's reflecting and reframing, he can begin to implement the *Touchstone Skills*, as well. "Tell me what you think we should do with the dogs?" "Is there something else that could be done?" The business owner might reply, "These dogs are bad for business and it takes away from income that could be focused on remedying this situation. This is a resort town and we rely on tourists who are too afraid to go on the beach because of the dog situation. I am really frustrated, because once we have a solution like capturing them, neutering and spaying them, and putting them up for adoption, that people then adopt them and let them go."

Now it is time for the individual with historical grief about the dogs to mirror back these sentiments as closely as possible so the businessman knows he understands the depth of his frustration. After this, some reframing statements by the individual with historical grief might include, "I understand you see that having these dogs running wild in the street and on the beach is hurting business and might be keeping tourists away. I also hear you say that you are very frustrated with those of us who are still caught up in past trauma and are releasing the dogs after adoption." This is where revealing emotions can help people build bridges of understanding by talking about their emotions and releasing the trauma that the historical grief individuals have transferred on to the dogs and the anxiety experienced by local business owners regarding their impact.

The *Touchstone Skills* and the *footstep processes* are precisely designed to foster movement away from debilitating emotions, such as anxiety and despair, toward the more empowering emotions, such as gratefulness and hopefulness. Although both positive and negative emotions may be experienced, if the balance can be shifted toward the more positive emotional pole, then less interpersonal distress will be experienced and there will be more room for negotiation around a mutually acceptable solution. As you may recall from Chapter One, empowerment is the process by which people gain mastery over issues of concern to them. Thus, the citizens of Constanta could gain empowerment when they find a way to work together to take charge of the situation and have direct influence on the decisions made around the wild dogs.

As you can see, the *Touchstone Skills* can be used in a variety to settings to help people work out compromises and create workable solutions. However, there will be times when these powerful communication tools are not a good match for the situation at hand. This might include acute or sudden conflicts where a third party is necessary to help those involved make decisions and resolve differences. In the next and final chapter, we will present such a situation and offer several options for third party interventions.

Chapter Seven
When the Dilemma Intensifies into Conflict:
Seeking Advice

Overview

This section of the book establishes guidelines for deciding when the *Touchstone Skills* and *footstep processes* can be effective without any outside assistance versus when you might consider bringing in an outside expert. We begin the chapter by bringing you back to the case scenario in Chapter Three concerning the plight of the Wild Mustangs. If there had been an impasse and working this out among themselves did not bring a resolution, they could bring in some outside assistance in the form of a mediator. We will take you through a brief overview of what the mediator, using the *InAccord* mediation model and *Touchstone Skills*, might be able to accomplish.

Following this, we return to the case of Karen and her supervisor and assume that there was no room for either negotiation or mediation in the process. In this case, we will describe what it would entail for Karen to go through the process of *arbitration*, which we will explain later in this chapter including the pros and cons of such a choice. Finally, we will discuss the alternative dispute resolution process of *restorative justice* and how it provides a venue for victims and offenders to find justice in criminal cases. The chapter concludes by requesting that you help us continue our research of the *Touchstone Skills* and *footstep processes*, by filling out a survey provided on our website in which you report on your ongoing experience as you walk this pathway to the resolution of everyday dilemmas and to self-liberation.

Assessing the Need for an Impartial Facilitator

The *Touchstone Skills*, enacted in addition to *footstep processes,* can be very effective in helping people resolve everyday dilemmas, including even challenging workplace disagreements. However, the individuals involved must first be able to calm their charged emotional responses, defuse historical factors that may be influencing their reactions, and learn to speak more constructively to those with whom they disagree. In cases of acute conflict or where people lack the ability to constructively engage with another, they can seek a neutral party to intervene. This can be as simple as asking a parent, religious leader, or friend to assist or by turning to a professional mediator to help the sides devise a collaborative solution that honors their shared interests. Sometimes, this decision will be intuitive and sometimes it calls for an evaluation of what factors might escalate the dilemma into a conflict that requires the expertise of an impartial party. Regardless, your journey thus far on the pathway, with the use of the *Touchstone Skills* and *footstep processes* will provide you with a strong, clarifying path as when you seek Mediation, Arbitration, or Restorative Justice.

Evaluating When to Use Mediation

As described above, there will be times when a dilemma within a family, another personal relationship, or a workplace dispute turns into an acute conflict and your own application of the *Touchstone Skills* will not be adequate to bring resolution. In this section, we present a decision-making chart that can help guide or inform you when it becomes necessary to discontinue the person-to- person use of the *Touchstone Skills* and seek outside guidance. You can opt for an informal choice as we mentioned above or hire a professional mediator, arbitrator, or restorative justice specialist. At Mediators Without Borders, we train each of these professionals to use the *InAccord Conflict Analysis®* model, following a process that uses the *Touchstone Skills* and measures disputant satisfaction and understanding at each step of the process employing our survey instruments.

In this section, we will return to the case of the Wild Mustangs and show how mediation can help when informal negotiations breakdown. First, we present a decision-making chart to help you determine when to use the *Touchstone Skills* on your own and when to refer the situation to an outside party, such as a mediator. It is important to know that by implementing the *InAccord* model of mediation you will still have control over the process. You will continue to follow a pathway that integrates all the *footstep processes*. Needing intervention or assistance with your dilemma is not a personal failure but a step on the journey to self-liberation as you learn additional skills to resolve your dilemmas during mediation sessions.

We have identified five categories of roadblocks in dilemmas where you can stop and consider whether to continue on your own or ask for assistance. These roadblocks include, (1) repetitive conflict issues arise; (2) the dilemma becomes overly complex; (3) stakes are high or highly sensitive; (4) dilemma is highly emotional; and/or (5) you need a referee. The table on the next page presents this evaluation as a decision-making process. In the left-hand column, we identify these roadblocks and in the middle describe the *Touchstone Skills* intervention you might employ on your own to resolve the dilemma. If this application to your own skills is not sufficient, we provide, in the right-hand column, a rationale for bringing in a mediator to help.

Table 3. Decision-Making Chart

Road Blocks	Touchstone Skills	Third Party Intervention
When either or all of the parties continue to repeat their concerns over and over again, it indicates that some issue is not being properly identified or some person is not feeling heard.	*At this point, you should return to reflecting until each party confirms that they feel heard by the other. You also need to return to questioning to see if there are any issues that are not being addressed.*	*If the conflict situation becomes repetitive over time, an informal or formal mediator can help you identify what issue is persisting and help you create solutions.*
When the dilemma is highly complex either in terms of the issues or the number of people involved.	*See if you can take one issue or work with one person at a time and make incremental progress and then assemble into larger and larger groups.*	*A mediator can help separate the issues into more workable units. He or she can also help manage a multi-party discussion or help you identify who should represent each group.*
Stakes are particularly high or dilemma is very sensitive.	*Explore your best alternative to negotiating this dilemma directly with the other by intra-psychic questioning, reflecting and reframing, first.*	*A mediator can set up rules of confidentiality, protect other interests (such as those of children) and help keep emotions in balance.*

Emotions continue to run high or there is a continued mismatch of emotions, meaning one party displays empowering emotions whereas the other is stuck in disempowering emotions	*If you have the highly emotional charge, move to the third party intervention; if you are calm and the other is charged, continue to reflect precisely what the other is saying, until they are cognitively clear what they need from you in order to continue.*	*A mediator can use private meetings, called caucuses, to help parties prevent their emotions from dominating the dialogue. Using the InAccord model, the mediator will assess from the My Feeling Surveys, if there is a mismatch of empowering and disempowering and make adjustments as called for.*
You cannot referee your own fight, don't know the rules, can't protect yourself, and/or need authority to initiate time outs.	*Use your intra-psychic Touchstone Skills to clarify your needs and desires in order to prepare for outside assistance.*	*A mediator can act as referee to maintain the rules of fair fighting, help each party act in their own best interests, and protect one party from another. They also know when to call a "time out"*

The Wild Mustangs: How Mediation Helps

In this case scenario, we return to the Wild Mustang case from Chapter Three. As you may recall the three involved were: 1) the rancher representative and 2) the head of the *Save the Mustang* group and 3) the horse specialist. They were able to move along the *footstep processes* along the Pathway implementing the *Touchstone Skills* effectively. Now let's assume a different scenario. None of these three people in the dispute had the skills or processes to calm their emotions evoked by the dilemma, and it quickly escalated into a conflict, punctuated by a shouting match between the Rancher Representative and Mustang Advocacy Representative. In this case, all three were so angry and disempowered that they could not identify any option except shouting and making their points with insults and threats. After about an hour of trying to get the two to stop shouting, the horse specialist declared the meeting over and recommended that the Bureau of Land Management hire a mediator to facilitate the dialogue to help everyone communicate more effectively.

The Bureau of Land Management (BLM) hired a mediator trained in the *InAccord* model and he suggested they all meet at his office because it was a neutral territory. At this first meeting, he began what is termed Phase One of the *InAccord* model by handing out the Conflict Styles, the My Feelings Survey (which is included Chapter Three of this book), along with a survey that assessed their expectations for the mediation. He spent some time reviewing these and noted that all three people involved reported feelings of anger, anxiety, and despair, which placed them squarely in the disempowered range. This informed the mediator to begin the meeting in a joint session where everyone could speak together about their concerns. It is important to note that, had there been a mismatch of emotions with one party feeling disempowered and the others empowered, he would have started the mediation with private meetings, shuttling between rooms to present ideas and issues for each of the three parties respectively.

The mediator began the preliminary session by setting ground rules that included no interruptions when another presented their perspective and ideas, no aggressive behavior in word or action, and an agreement to work collaboratively on a joint solution. These were all included in a document called The Agreement to Mediate, which each party signed at the outset. The mediator then began to instruct the three individuals in how to use the *Touchstone Skills* from the *InAccord* model, in the first caucus or private meeting. He let them know that he would be helping them throughout the process to refine these skills in order to reach a resolution.

At this point, the mediator began to take the three individuals, the rancher representative, the head of the *Save the Mustang* group, and the horse expert/specialist through the 4 stages of *InAccord* mediation, which we refer to as Phase Two of the model. In the first stage, the parties shared their perspectives of the dilemma and the mediator wrote down the initial issues, positions, and interests that emerged from the sharing of each party. The mediator had the three individuals share their stories about the dilemma, their fears about what might happen to the wild horses, and their ideas about what their ultimate goal would be. At the conclusion of this stage, each person filled out a survey that assessed their understanding and satisfaction with the process thus far. The mediator then reviewed their responses to determine if they were ready to move on to the next stage or needed more time to clarify or understand certain interests or issues that came up.

If the parties were ready to move on, they would begin the second stage of developing an agenda and generating options for resolving the dilemma. In this stage, they are encouraged to begin to brainstorm, identifying any and all options and assembling these into specific solutions for discussion. The three individuals came up with a long list of options that included relocating the horses, making adoption of the mustangs easier for the public, exploring birth control options for both mares and stallions, and allowing the BLM to euthanize horses that were injured or starving to death. At the conclusion, they each filled out a survey to ensure they understood and were satisfied with this stage of the process.

The next stage of the mediation process involves the creation of a joint solution statement, drawing upon the issues and many options generated in the previous stage. The three individuals began to develop shared agreements based on their individual interests and tested them in reality by constructing how they might be implemented and what obstructions might be encountered. For instance, they created a strategy for a birth control initiative and then tested it by examining how much this might cost, where funds for this process could be generated, what kind of manpower would be needed to administer the process, which groups would provide the money and manpower, and what kind of timeline this might involve. This stage can include a great deal of bargaining and trading options as they work together to create final options. For instance, the head of the mustang group agreed to concentrate more fundraising dollars on a birth control strategy, if the BLM would impose fines on people who adopted horses and then sold them for slaughter. The representative for the ranchers agreed to approach his group for funds for birth control, if the advocacy group would agree to share the cost and if the BLM would ease up on adoption requirements for the public. As in the other stages, they concluded by filling out the satisfaction and understanding surveys before moving on to the next stage.

The final stage is the creation of a contract, called a Memorandum of Agreement (MOA), which serves to guide parties in their implementation of joint solutions. In this case, the agreement began with a joint statement that read, "In the spirit of cooperation and serving the best interests of America's Wild Mustangs, we hereby agree to the following:" After this statement, the MOA listed the specifics of the joint solution that the three agreed upon. Given that they would each need to return to their respective groups for approval, the MOA included a timeline for a second meeting with the mediator to either sign the agreement or re-negotiate if the groups have amendments or changes they would like their representatives to present. The parties each filled out a final satisfaction and understanding survey which the mediator reviewed to ensure they were ready to sign the MOA.

At the end of Phase Two, comprised of the 4 stages, the mediator initiates the third and final phase of Post-Facilitation Outcomes. In this phase, the mediator directs each party to fill out the Exit Survey which measures their overall understanding of and satisfaction with the *InAccord* model of mediation as well as the fairness and impartiality of the mediator. In addition, they rate the extent to which the process was transparent and empowering. Finally, each party fills out the Post My Feelings Survey and Expectations scale to assess whether there has been a change in the intensity of feelings or if their expectations of saving time and money as well were met. The following table provides an overview of the *InAccord* mediation phases and stages and surveys that are included in each phase and stage.

Table 4: Overview of Phases and Associated Surveys to assess the InAccord Mediation Model

PHASE ONE Pre-Facilitation Assessment	PHASE TWO 4 Stage Intervention Scores	PHASE THREE Post-Facilitation Outcomes
Conflict Styles Survey* -Avoidance - Competition -Compromise -Accommodation -Collaboration **My Feelings Pre Survey*** -Empowering Feelings -Disempowering Feelings *My Expectations Survey** -Saving money -Saving time -Saving the relationship	*Stage 1: Sharing of Perspectives: Issues, Positions, and Interest Identification***(caucus; review touchstone skill sets) - Understanding - Satisfaction *Stage 2: Developing the Agenda and Option Generation*** -Understanding -Satisfaction *Stage 3: Joint Solution Statements: Testing the Agreements in Principle*** -Understanding -Satisfaction *Stage 4: Crafting the MOA ** -Understanding -Satisfaction	*Signed versus did not sign* *Exit Survey*** - InAccord Model successful, party satisfied -Can understand, implement InAccord Model -Mediator fair/impartial -Process transparent -Process empowering *My Feelings Post Survey** -Empowering Feelings -Disempowering Feelings *My Expectations Survey** -Saved money -Saved time -Saved the relationship

*Mediator evaluates disputant responses to survey **Mediator completes a parallel version of this survey

Evaluating when to use Arbitration

Arbitration is the submission of a dispute for resolution to a private, unofficial person outside of the courts, selected as provided by agreement of the parties in the dispute. Most cases filed in US court systems never make it to trial. For instance, in the Federal Court that sits in Denver, Colorado, less than 3% of all cases filed actually proceed to trial. That means that 97% of all cases are either dismissed or settled. While settlement through mediation tends to save a future, ongoing relationship and is undoubtedly the most cost-effective means for bringing a dispute to final resolution, some disputes simply cannot be settled. In these cases, arbitration may offer an attractive alternative to litigation in the court systems. This is particularly true when there is no anticipation of an ongoing relationship between the parties.

The major difference between mediation and arbitration is who renders the decision; in arbitration, a third party (the arbitrator) decides the final outcome, whereas in mediation (if there is resolution), the parties involved in the dispute mutually agree upon the final outcome. Arbitration is typically far less expensive and time consuming than litigation, but it does not necessarily insure satisfied parties. According to the National Association of Realtors Arbitration Work Group, "Arbitration is by nature a somewhat confrontational, adversarial, 'win/lose' process. Non-prevailing parties [those who lose the case] remain convinced of their entitlement; prevailing parties resent having to participate in arbitration to be 'awarded' what they view as rightfully theirs."

Mediation can be a more satisfying process for many parties to a dispute. First, it is always voluntary, allowing parties the chance to step away from the table at any point in time. Second, mediation requires that the parties actively participate in the process and craft their own solution. The parties control the outcome. The parties to the dispute make the decision, and only they can render it final through entering into an executed written agreement, enforceable as a legally binding contract. The mediator has no authority to render a binding decision. The arbitrator, however, does. Table 5 provides an overview of the major differences between these two types of dispute resolution.

Table 5. The Contrast between Mediation and Arbitration

Characteristics of the Process	Arbitration	Mediation
The source of decision-making authority	Parties decide to submit their dispute to arbitration (often through contractual arbitration clause). Once parties agree to arbitration, their agreement is binding.	Parties mutually agree to take dispute to mediation or may be court mandated. However, mediation is always voluntary. Even court mandated mediation requires only that the parties participate, not that they reach agreement.
	Parties choose the state or city where the arbitration is to occur. Actual location of the hearing is in a neutral location.	Often takes place in neutral territory
	Arbitrators decide the disputes submitted to them	Mediators decide whether or not to take cases submitted to them
	Decisions made by arbitrator(s)	Decision made by parties
	Rarely can be appealed	Parties can decide not to settle
Procedure	Confidential	Confidential
	Adversarial	Goal is to be Cooperative (process can often be adversarial)
	Flexible process	Flexible process
	Parties choose the "rules of the game"	Parties and mediators determine ground rules
Characteristics of third party involved	Arbitrators are selected by the parties	Parties select a mediator
	Arbitrators can be experts in particular fields or areas of law	Mediators are process experts, may or may not be substance experts
	Arbitration panels can include	Mediators can be outsider-

	partial as well as non-partial arbitrators or one non-partial arbitrator	neutrals or insider partials. If insider partials, they often work with an outsider-neutral.
Type of Result	Parties can determine an end date (fast track arbitration)	Ends once cooperative agreement is reached, or parties decide not to settle
	Typically Win-lose solution	Win-win solutions or No Result
Enforcement	National regulations provide enforcement mechanism Without a binding treaty; International arbitrations may lack an enforcement mechanism.	Implementation of agreement depends largely on the parties' good will, but the court may enforce in some circumstances.
	Award conclusive, final and binding (right of appeal is very limited)	No appeal once settled; another process can be used if no settlement is reached

InAccord Arbitration: Empirically Designed, Disputant Focused

Arbitration is used widely in the United States and abroad as an alternative to litigation, initially designed to save both money and time for those involved in a dispute. However, over time, arbitration has become a very costly process and one that is under increasing public scrutiny due to rather blatant conflicts of interest within some large arbitration-sponsoring organizations. The issues of fairness and transparency have been under great scrutiny by certain public interest groups, particularly when arbitration is "forced" as part of a binding contract. This is the case with many credit card companies, banks, cell providers, computer manufacturers, cable and internet providers, brokerages, and home builders. In 2009, Public Citizen, a leading consumer advocacy group published a critical report examining the widespread use of forced arbitration by these select industries. The report illustrated the abuses of a system they believed was created by and for industry where evidence has revealed a highly un-level playing field between the industries and the consumers they serve.

The inequity between industries and their consumers is due, in part, to the select designation in many contracts of a single sponsoring organization that will be employed in all arbitrations. A sponsoring organization provides rules and procedures that are followed in arbitration and often provide the arbitrators directly through their organization or through a referral network. Many times when you sign a workplace contract, you will see an arbitration clause that specifies that only a certain such organization is to be selected. What makes this process subject to abuse is that these organizations have a direct business contract with the industry for which they are providing the arbitration services. This, in turn, makes impartiality and fairness to the consumer in a dispute very difficult, especially if there is no mechanism to track the efficacy of the process and the perceived fairness by both industry representatives and consumers. In contrast, Mediators Without Borders is a sponsoring organization of arbitration that uses the *InAccord Conflict Analysis®* model to carefully track the feelings of disputants before and after the process as well as their understanding and satisfaction with the process along the way. In this manner, one can track both the overall effectiveness of the model as well as the perceived impartiality and fairness of the arbitrator who facilitates the process.

Karen and Terrell: Using the InAccord Arbitration Process

We now return to the case of Karen, covered in Chapter Five on using the *Touchstone Skills*. She worked as a paramedic at an ambulance company. Recall that she had heard rumors that she would be passed over for a promotion, in favor of a younger male applicant. Unlike the previous scenario, in this version of the case, Karen met with Terrell, her supervisor, who told her that this was a company decision and she had to simply accept their choice. There was no room for discussion, negotiation, or explanation; therefore, Karen decided to seek arbitration as was called for in her employment contract which had been renewed the previous year. The contract specified several arbitration sponsors that Karen could choose and she selected Mediators Without Borders and an *InAccord* arbitrator. Table 6 on the following page, outlines the specific phases and stages of this model as well as the survey instruments used at each Phase and Stage to assess the efficacy of the process, including client satisfaction and understanding. These will be explained employing Karen's arbitration as a sample case.

Table 6: Overview of Phases, Stages, and Associated Surveys of the InAccord Arbitration Model

PHASE ONE Preliminary Conference	PHASE TWO 3 Stages of the Hearing	PHASE THREE Post-Hearing Outcomes
Arbitration Demand - issued by complainant *Preliminary Meeting* -with all parties present *My Expectations Scale** -Award in their favor -Saving time versus litigation -Saving money versus litigation -Arbitration will be procedurally fair - Arbitrator will be fair - Necessary evidence and witnesses will be available -Process will be transparent & empowering *Touchstone Skills* -Communication rules -Review three skills	*Stage 1: Opening Statements and/or Pre-hearing documents* *Stage 1 Understanding and Satisfaction Survey** - Understanding - Satisfaction *Stage 2: Witnesses and Testimony* *Stage 2 Understanding and Satisfaction Survey** -Understanding -Satisfaction *Stage 3: Closing Statements* *Stage 3 Understanding and Satisfaction Survey** -Understanding -Satisfaction	*Rendering of the Award* *Motions to Vacate Award* *My Expectations Exit Survey** -Award in their favor -Saving time versus litigation -Saving money versus litigation -Arbitration was procedurally fair - Arbitrator was fair - Necessary evidence and witnesses were available -Process was transparent & empowering

Preliminary Discovery -Document submissions -List of witnesses -Expected testimony -Any subpoenas -Translator needed -Site visits *Phase One Understanding &Satisfaction Survey*		

*Arbitrator evaluates disputant responses to survey and completes a parallel version of this survey

Karen issued an arbitration demand to the arbitrator which outlined for her the basis of her claim and the amount of damages she was seeking. Upon review of the claim, the arbitrator had her assistant contact each party to set up a prehearing conference to present and discuss the case. It is important to note that an arbitrator, as opposed to a mediator, must never have direct contact with either party alone but always include both in any discussions. Karen and the company representative met at the arbitrator's office for the conference and the arbitrator began Phase One by issuing each party the *My Expectations Survey* which measures the parties' expectations of whether the process will (1) be awarded in their favor, (2) will save them time versus litigation, (3) will save them money in contrast to litigation, and (4) will be a procedurally fair process. Additionally, the *My Expectations Survey* will measure whether each party expects the arbitrator to be impartial, expects to have the necessary evidence assembled for the case, and expects that the list of witnesses will be present when called.

At the outset, in Phase One, the arbitrator explains that there are three phases to the *InAccord* arbitration process: (1) Preliminary Conference, (2) the Hearing Process, and (3) Post-Hearing Outcomes. The arbitrator then explains that the first phase will include her explanation of the entire process and the submission by each party of the *My Expectations Surveys*. Once this process occurs, the *InAccord* arbitrator details the manner of communication that is acceptable between the arbitrator, the parties, and any attorneys that might be involved in the case.

In the Phase One preliminary conference, ground rules are set for the dialogue. The *InAccord* arbitrator extrapolates the issues (the reasons they are seeking arbitration), positions (what each disputant would like to see happen), and interests (why each disputant is taking the position he/she is taking), while tracking the differing perspectives. In many instances, the parties are hearing one another's perspectives for the first time as well as feeling the weight of the process that lay before them. Sometimes, this sharing period will result in one or both parties agreeing not to continue to the hearing phase but either submit the case to mediation or to a settlement conference, which is a meeting between the parties themselves and/or their attorneys. In this case, the arbitrator would leave the proceedings and let the settlement conference occur without her or refer the case to an *InAccord* mediator. The arbitrator would never be in the settlement conference nor should he or she assume the new role of mediator.

During Phase One, the arbitrator suggests that each party set up a prehearing *discovery* process which includes a timeline for submissions of documents, lists of witnesses and expected testimony, subpoenas (if necessary), and translators (if necessary). This discovery process is not required in arbitration, but it can save considerable expense if it is done prior to the actual hearing. Once this process is outlined, it can result in a settlement conference or mediation as the parties see how lengthy and expensive the process might be. Once these details are adequately addressed, the arbitrator issues a written pre-hearing order which outlines what each party has agreed to, including what dates they have selected for submission of each discovery issue. For instance, in Karen's case, she has witnesses from work that she would like to have interviewed to substantiate her claim that the company is discriminatory against women employees. She also requested a record of the company hiring practices and promotions for the last ten years. The pre-hearing order outlines when the witnesses will be available and when the company will have the records available for the arbitrator.

In Karen's case, a settlement conference might result in the company attorneys agreeing to a settlement amount if Karen agrees to drop the charge of gender discrimination and agree to a lesser claim. In this way, Karen can either receive a monetary settlement claim or a promotion to supervisor while the company avoids opening itself to an admission of sexual discrimination. Both parties could also agree to complete confidentiality of the proceedings in order to avoid public scrutiny of the settlement terms. The arbitrator concludes this phase by issuing the *Phase One Survey* that captures disputants' understanding of and satisfaction with this Phase.

The arbitrator will review the final surveys in Phase One to determine if the parties understand everything that was presented and are satisfied with the process. If they are ready and desire to move into a formal hearing, the arbitrator will set the dates for Phase Two, the Hearing Process. In this case, the *InAccord* arbitrator will set the dates to allow enough time for the submission of all the preliminary discovery items. Again, the parties can choose to abandon the hearing phase at any time before or during the hearing in order to decide matters in conference or through *InAccord* mediation.

The hearing itself is much like a court hearing without the formality of a traditional court and with the added benefit of complete confidentiality. Stage 1 of the hearing begins with formal swearing in of both Karen and the company representative and then Karen's attorney is instructed to provide an opening statement followed by a statement from the attorney for the company. Any evidence not provided in the discovery phase can be submitted during this stage of the hearing. At the conclusion of the opening statements, the parties are instructed to complete an understanding and satisfaction survey to ensure they are ready to move on. The arbitrator reviews these and then determines if they are prepared to move to Stage 2.

Stage 2 of the hearing involves witnesses and testimony. In Karen's case, her attorney may call witnesses such as co-workers who have relevant information about the case. The company attorney may cross-examine these witnesses and the arbitrator may ask pertinent questions as well. This is followed by the company attorney calling witnesses who are then cross-examined by Karen's attorney and the arbitrator. Rebuttal witnesses may be called during this stage of the hearing as may expert witnesses who can provide relevant information pertaining to the case. At the end of witness testimony, the parties are again instructed to complete understanding and satisfaction surveys which the arbitrator reviews in order to determine if they are prepared to move to Stage 3.

Stage 3 of the hearing phase ends with closing statements by both attorneys where they summarize the evidence and testimony and present their final arguments for their clients. Upon conclusion of the closing arguments, the arbitrator issues the understanding and satisfaction survey for stage 3 of the arbitration hearing. It is important to note that, at any time during these three stages of the hearing, the parties may ask for a settlement conference or mediation rather than an arbitration award.

The final phase of the *InAccord* arbitration process involves the Post-Hearing outcomes which includes the award, any moves to vacate or cancel the award, and the submission of the *My Expectations Exit Survey* completed by both Karen and the company representative. These are kept by the arbitrator as part of an anonymous aggregation of surveys across disputants and integrated into a research study into the effectiveness of the model. The *InAccord* arbitration process is binding, meaning that the parties must comply with the terms of the award. There can be grounds to vacate an award but this is very rare and claimants must show either (a) corruption or fraud in the proceedings, (b) partiality by the arbitrator, (c) excessive use of arbitrator power, or (d) and arbitrator mandate of a hearing before all evidence can be reasonably submitted. For those who need to decide between arbitration and litigation, the contrast between arbitration and litigation is more fully explained in the book *In Justice, in Accord* (Ries & Harter, 2012).

Evaluating when to use InAccord Restorative Justice

Restorative Justice, often simply referred to as "RJ", is a term that encompasses a growing list of alternatives to "retributive" justice systems around the world. In general, it is an approach to justice that focuses on the needs of the victim, the offender, and the larger community that is affected by a crime. The victim is encouraged to take an active role in the restorative justice process while offenders are encouraged to repair the harm they have done through apology, compensation, and/or community service.

For example, there is a case of an adolescent who had been drinking, stole a golf cart and drove it into a tree. Clearly he offended the owners of the golf cart and he was referred to a Mediators Without Borders RJ Program. In the pre-conference, this adolescent admitted fault and in his *My Feelings Survey* checked "Very Strong" when it came to the emotion of "Guilt". Those who were victimized wanted not only an apology, but felt "Anger" in their survey and wanted their golf cart restored to its original condition. The adolescent, in the spirit of making restitution to the victims, both apologized and agreed to pay for the golf cart to be fixed.

Restorative justice is based on the theory of procedural justice and considers criminal acts to be offenses against individuals and communities rather than the state or country. Restorative justice promotes four processes, (1) mutual respect that recognizes the humanity of the other; (2) collaboration and working together to find solutions; (3) a completely voluntary process that allows all parties to decide whether or not to participate; and (4) the empowerment of all parties by providing the tools and space to develop solutions to their own problems. However, at this point, we caution: *There may be cases where serious criminal activity is involved that may not be suitable for RJ and requires thoughtful, appropriate intervention to ensure an individual's Human Rights or a case that may be subject to a criminal investigation, that involves Legal Rights.*

Restorative justice processes vary across jurisdictions in the United States and abroad; however, involvement of victim, offender and community, where possible, is encouraged in most cases. According to Sherman and Strang (2007), restorative justice that fosters dialogue between the victim and the offender demonstrates the highest rates of victim satisfaction and offender accountability. The *InAccord* Restorative Justice specialist is a trained *InAccord* mediator and arbitrator who facilitates a process that allows for assessments of effectiveness, understanding, and satisfaction. For this reason, we will refer to the specialist as an RJ facilitator even though his or her background includes mediation and arbitration training and experience as well. The actual process can be divided into three Phases: preliminary conference, conference, and post-conference follow-up. Phase One in the *InAccord* RJ model, is referred to as the preliminary conference because it helps the RJ facilitator to assess whether Restorative Justice is appropriate for the case and it prepares all parties to the crime for the actual conference in Phase Two. The preliminary conference begins with the *InAccord* RJ facilitator meeting with the victim and offender separately to ensure they understand the process. The parties are asked to invite the support people whom they wish to attend the actual conference. In the offender meeting, the facilitator defines the expectations and commitments that the offender must make to participate in the process. These include a willingness to engage in authentic and open dialogue about the offense including what happened, how it happened, and why it happened. This preliminary meeting includes a discussion of what might be required to make things just or fair as possible for the victim, including restitutions, community service, and/or an apology. It also requires that the offender commit to a discussion and agreement on how to prevent a re-occurrence of the event in the future. This alone time with the offender affords the *InAccord* RJ facilitator a chance to evaluate the earnestness with which the offender is approaching the conferencing. The meeting with the victim also focuses on a discussion of the crime and its impact on the victim, including the needs of the victim or the victim's family.

Both victims and offenders are asked to fill out the *My Feeling Pre Survey* and the *My Expectations Survey* in the initial phase of the process. If the offender is in a more empowered state than the victim, as measured by the survey results, the Restorative Justice facilitator will recommend that the process begin as a directive approach rather than using restorative justice conferencing. This decision is made to protect the victim from any re-traumatization from an offender who may not be serious about taking responsibility and making amends for the crime. On the other hand, if the offender is disempowered and the victim is empowered, the *InAccord* RJ facilitator can move ahead with the conferencing phase. This is also true if both offender and victim are in either a disempowered state or empowered state. Phase Two of the RJ process encompasses the conference between the victim and offender and members of the community that might have been affected. A central function of the conferencing phase is to convey disapproval of the *behavior* while showing regard for the offender as a person. The overall goal of this process is to help the offender re-integrate into society while honoring the victim's need to have their experience validated. The conference begins with the *InAccord* RJ facilitator going over the *Touchstone Skills* which are used in the process. Additionally, they review ground rules such as no name calling, no interruptions, and no threatening behavior or words.

Stage 1 of Phase Two, consists of sharing perspectives about the crime. The dialogue begins with the victim choosing who goes first the victim or the offender. The party selected proceeds to talk about the events of the crime, its impact, and the feelings they have in regard to the offense. After this person has completed his or her perspective, the other party engages in the same process and then they are encouraged to engage the *Touchstone Skills* by asking one another questions, reflecting back the answers, and reframing where appropriate. The RJ facilitator is on hand to guide these discussions should the dialogue become destructive to the overall process of the restoration of both victim and offender. Stage 1 also involves an acknowledgement of the supporters of the victim and supporters of the offender who are each encouraged to talk about how the crime impacted them personally. The victim's supporters have an opportunity to express their perceptions of the overall impact of the crime. The offender's supporters share their own viewpoints, including any knowledge that might help others understand the offender and the motives for the crime.

Stage Two, the Conference Phase, begins when the sharing of perspectives has concluded and the RJ facilitator asks an open-ended question to the victim and offender about what would need to happen to right the wrong of the act that was committed. The victim usually begins the dialogue listing the losses or damages incurred and the facilitator assists a dialogue between victim and offender as to how to make amends for these losses. The RJ facilitator begins to list possible options and facilitates a discussion about which choices are feasible and how each would be implemented. The final decisions made in Stage 2 of the Phase Two conference, are memorialized (a legal term) or concretized in an agreement that both parties sign at the end of the final stage of Phase Two.

Stage 3 of this phase includes a discussion about how the offender plans to alter their behavior in ways that will prevent further criminal acts and help them re-integrate into the community. This might include education, community service, addiction counseling, anger management, or re-employment. These changes are also included in the final agreement document signed by both parties. The conference concludes with each party filling out the My Feelings Post Survey, the My Expectations Exit survey, and Stage Three Understanding and Satisfaction Survey.

Phase Three of the process consists of a post-conference follow-up which includes monitoring the agreement that was established in the conference to ensure compliance by the offender. The post-conference also includes two follow-up phone calls or live meetings at 3 months and 6 months after the conference. This would occur between the mediator and each of the party's individually, in order to track levels of empowerment, understanding, and satisfaction over time. At each meeting, both party's communicated to the mediator any progress and challenges. Each party then fills out the *My Feelings Post Survey*, the *My Expectations Exit survey*, and the post conference *Understanding and Satisfaction Surveys*. The *InAccord* Restorative Justice process is highlighted in Table 7 on the following page.

Table 7: Overview of Phases, Stages, and Associated Surveys of the InAccord Restorative Justice Model

PHASE ONE Preliminary Conference	PHASE TWO 3 Stages of the Conference	PHASE THREE Post-Conference Outcomes
Preliminary Meeting -with all parties present *My Feelings Pre Survey** -Empowering Feelings -Disempowering Feelings *My Expectations Scale** -RJ Process will be procedurally fair - Facilitator will be fair - Supporters will be heard -Process will be transparent & empowering	*Stage 1: Sharing of Perspectives* *-Touchstone Skills Overview* -Communication rules -Review three skills -Victim/Offender perspectives -Supporters perspectives *Stage 1 Understanding and Satisfaction Survey** - Understanding - Satisfaction *Stage 2: Amends and MOA* -facilitated discussion of solutions -Creation of written agreement *Stage 2 Understanding and Satisfaction Survey** -Understanding -Satisfaction *Stage 3: Offender Reconciliation* -re-integration commitments	*Monitoring Compliance* *3 Month Meeting* *My Feelings Post Survey** -Empowering Feelings -Disempowering Feelings *My Expectations Exit Survey** - RJ Process will be procedurally fair - Facilitator will be fair - Supporters will be heard -Process will be transparent & empowering *6 Month Meeting* *My Feelings Post Survey** -Empowering Feelings -Disempowering

	Stage 3 Understanding and Satisfaction Survey* -Understanding -Satisfaction	Feelings *My Expectations Exit Survey** - RJ Process will be procedurally fair - Facilitator will be fair - Supporters will be heard -Process will be transparent & empowering

*Facilitator evaluates disputant responses to survey and completes a parallel version of this survey

The Importance of Research in Evaluating the Efficacy of the InAccord Mediation Model

Much of the initial evidence for the effectiveness of the *InAccord* model of mediation has come from the clinical and mediational experience of the first author, Ries. The accumulating evidence through these mediation interventions with couples, family, companies, and countries provides a powerful demonstration of the efficacy of the model, on a case-by-case basis. However, we have moved toward a more systematic, empirical documentation of the effectiveness of the *InAccord* model, employing appropriate research designs and statistical techniques (Ries & Harter, 2012).

Three patterns of findings stand out that may interest the reader of this volume. First, the authors have documented the importance of identifying the emotions that people bring to a dilemma or conflict, particularly charting change as a function of the implementation of the *Touchstone Skills*, based on surveys like the one you filled out in this book. What they documented through participant surveys was that those, in mediation training, who employed the *Touchstone Skills* of Questioning, Reflecting, and Reframing, reported that their emotions

178

were altered, as a result. The positive empowering emotions increased in frequency, whereas the disempowering emotions declined in frequency, one index of the effectiveness of the intervention. The second pattern of findings, documented through additional surveys, revealed that participants *understood* both the principles and concepts to which they have also been introduced. Moreover, they reported high levels of *satisfaction* with what they had learned that could be applied to their own relational lives. The third pattern of findings spoke to the participant's overall evaluation of the mediation intervention. In an exit survey, they reported (a)that the *InAccord* model was very successful, leading to their personal satisfaction; (b) that they fully understood the principles and how they could be implemented; (c) that their specific expectations were realized, and (d) that the mediator was fair and impartial. Thus, there is solid evidence for the efficacy of employing the *InAccord model* within the context of restorative justice, should you eventually decide on such an option. Based on Ries and Harter's findings, we took the next step to see if we could impart these principles to people whose relationships were *not* in acute conflict, but who faced the inevitable decision-making demands and problem-solving tasks in any normal relationship.

Future Research on the Processes Presented in This Volume

We are now planning to conduct further research on the communication skills we have described in this book where we have taken a somewhat different tact in that the skills are designed to be more *preventative* in nature. A major goal is to prevent dilemmas from mushrooming into acute conflicts. The two primary features have been first, that the focus be on the inevitable day-to-day dilemmas that people face in their lives, *not* acute conflicts, and secondly, that people can apply and practice the communication skills on their own, with those also involved in the dilemma.

New to this volume is a theoretical model developed by the first author, Ries, which identifies a pathway of processes, conceptualized

179

as a circle, toward two primary goals. The first more proximal objective is the *resolution* of a given dilemma. The deeper, more psychological goal is to foster people's growth toward a greater feeling of self-liberation. The processes that define this circle of communication, defined as footsteps along the pathway, were depicted in Table 1, presented in the Introduction, and described in the text that followed.

It should be noted that our next research efforts will involve an examination of this theoretical model through the use of rigorous research practices. It is our goal to bring such methodologies to bear upon the validity of the new model, demonstrating its efficacy. Certain processes that we identify in this circle *have* been the object of research scrutiny in our first volume (Ries & Harter, 2013), for example the role of "revealing emotions", "empowerment," "transparency," as well an understanding of, and satisfaction with, the Touchstone Skills. Other newly described processes in the current book will be the object of subsequent research.

For example, what has yet to be empirically examined is the validity of the model in its entirety. That is, does the order of the footsteps, the processes along the circle, hold up under research scrutiny? To take another example (depicted in the circle), does revealing emotions, coupled with a sense of empowerment, actually facilitate people's ability to gain perspective (taking the perspective of others, sharing perspectives, and shifting one's perspective)? Does gaining perspective, in turn, lead to the ability to engage in empathy and compassion? Are transparency and authenticity a natural prerequisite to the resolution of the dilemma and to self-liberation? How do the *Touchstones Skills* facilitate the *footsteps processes* along the pathway that defines the circle? These are the types of questions that our next wave of research will address.

Toward this goal, we are going to ask you to help us, the authors, by sharing your own insights. We have one last anonymous survey that we would like to submit to us, it would be very helpful and instructive to obtain your input. This survey will be placed on line at the following website: Readily understandable instructions will be provided on the webpage. We thank you in advance for your cooperation. We very much value your insights and are grateful to you for providing them to us. Findings from the on-line survey will be presented in the second edition of this book.

Conclusion

At its heart, the practice of the *Touchstone Skills* and *footstep processes* address self-talk and interpersonal exchanges between people (be they friends, couples, or family members); within *companies* (between colleagues or between employers and employees); or in international relations (between or within countries) where issues of cultural sensitivity, compassion, and gaining perspective become all the more critical. In each case, there is an attempt to both understand and be understood by individuals and within groups. Our goal has been to enable you, the reader, to share with others your own perspective in a way that aids the others in understanding who you are, what you want, and perhaps who you are seeking to become. Equally as important, the pathway offers you the ability to appreciate what others want and need and who they are seeking to become. In this way, both perspectives are enriched, perceived differently, and *questioned/reflected/reframed* as we build a community one person at a time and learn to walk a shared pathway of increased understanding and humility.

This book is a personal journey. When you initiate your journey along the path, combining both the *Touchstone Skills* and *footstep processes*, you will experience a profound shift in your perceptions of clarity and purpose. Inevitably, you will find yourself mired in everyday dilemmas, much like a hamster on a wheel, going round and round from one problem to the next with no clear resolution in sight. At other times, you will be tempted to be lulled into dilemmas and situations that lead you down a predictable, yet undesirable path. This happened one degree at a time, as you automatically avoid the tough conversations and accept life on life's terms, no longer in touch with the negative emotional states that are influencing you. Now, as a result of learning the *Touchstone Skills* and *footstep processes*, these negative states can functions as indicators that you have strayed off the pathway.

At its heart, the *Touchstone Skills* of questioning, reflecting, and reframing, is designed to provide you, the reader, with insights about

183

how you approach a difficult situation or interpersonal challenges in the future. As we stated in the introduction, when Ries completed her first book with Harter, *In Justice, InAccord*, she knew there was another volume in waiting, a text that would present a more preventative narrative of how to avoid the escalation of a dilemma. We sought to address the *Touchstone Skills* necessary to deal with everyday problem-solving and decision-making situations. Indeed, we began almost immediately on our *Touchstones* text with a greater focus on how to apply the *Touchstone Skills* of questioning, reflecting and reframing and the *InAccord* pillars of revealing emotions, empowerment, gaining perspective, empathy/compassion, transparency and authenticity, so critical to change and self-liberation when faced with challenging situations. It is this *pathway*, combining both the skills and theory that we offer to you.

In working on this volume, we each experienced our own individual and collective transformation and it is our hope the same may happen to you along this journey. It is this combination of integration of the *footstep processes and Touchstone Skills* that continue to loosen the grip our old ways of thinking that may longer serve us. It is our intention to follow the pathway to improve everyday life and quench our yearning for honesty, directness, and sincerity, while maintaining and understanding the need for humility and kindness, in an attempt to reveal the authentic self. Thus, there is a higher-order principle embedded into the Mediators Without Borders culture of *do no harm* in our interactions.

As a team and in our day-to-day actions, we leave you with a *practice* that seeks to build connectedness and care during a time that the world is desperately seeking for solutions to the divide that separates us. This work builds upon our research into the psychological foundations of our *InAccord Conflict Analysis* model. We, as a cohesive group, want to impart the importance of the twin flames of authenticity and transparency, yours and ours. We believe self-liberation is a building block for more appropriate interpersonal conversations, inner congruency and a solid footing. We understand that we are standing at the beginning of this theoretical model and look to your insights and wisdom as we continue our research and offer our findings.

An Invitation to our Readers

We would appreciate it if you would provide us with what would be valuable feedback on our framework labeled A Theoretical Pathway to Self-Liberation, captured in Figure 1, which we have reproduced for you on the following page. Your responses will be particularly helpful to our future research and critical to documenting the foundations of this framework. Your insights will help us in our ongoing mission to keep our model current and responsive to those facing every day dilemmas. Please review the circular pathway figure provided below where we suggest that each feature of the circle impacts the next. After you have a chance to review, please link to our website and print out and mail back the form. We appreciate your willingness to help us continue refining our work. The survey questions are provided in this book as well, following the figure of the circular pathway.

A Theoretical Pathway to Self-Liberation

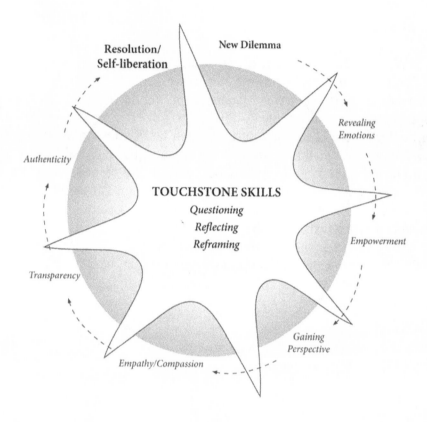

1. To what extent do you feel that the *footsteps of* Revealing Emotions and Empowerment are essential prerequisites that facilitate your movement to the footstep of Gaining Perspective, which includes taking others' perspective, sharing perspectives with others, and shifting your own perspective? That is: How true is this for you in your own experience of dealing with a specific dilemma in your everyday life? (Circle Just One.)

Very True   Pretty True   Not Very True   Not at All True

Please provide a brief example from a dilemma in your own life.

How have any of the *Touchstone Skills* in the middle of the circle (Questioning, Reflecting, or Reframing) been useful in moving you from Revealing Emotions and Empowerment to Gaining Perspective, given the dilemma you reported above? Describe how these skills worked for you.

2. To what extent do you feel that applying the footstep of Gaining Perspective (in the circle) helps you become more Empathic and Compassionate toward others in a dilemma. That is, how *true* is this for *you* in your own experience of a particular dilemma? (Circle Just One).

Very True   Pretty True   Not Very True   Not at All True

Please give us a brief example, based on the dilemma you are reporting.

How have any of the *Touchstone Skills* in the middle of the circle (Questioning, Reflecting, or Reframing) been useful in moving you from Gaining Perspective to feeling more Empathic and Compassionate toward others, given the dilemma you reported above?

3. The circle suggests that once you experience the *footsteps* of Empathy and Compassion for another it will enhance both your process of Transparency and your own expression of Authenticity. How *true* is this for *you* in your own experience of dealing with a particular dilemma in everyday life? (Circle Just One.)

    Very True   Pretty True   Not Very True   Not at All True

Please provide a brief example based on the dilemma you are reporting.

4. Finally, we have suggested that developing the *footsteps* of Transparency and Personal Authenticity will enhance your ability to Resolve a given dilemma and facilitate your movement toward greater Self-Liberation. How TRUE is this for YOU in your own experience of dealing with a particular dilemma in your everyday life? (Circle Just One.)

    Very True   Pretty True   Not Very   True Not at All True

Please provide a brief example of how your response applies to the particular dilemma you are reporting?

How have any of the *Touchstone Skills* in the middle of the circle (Questioning, Reflecting, or Reframing) been useful in moving you from Transparency and Personal Authenticity to Resolution of the dilemma you described and thus facilitated your movement toward greater Self-Liberation?

Now that you have been through the material in the volume, what does Self-Liberation mean to you personally?

Please submit your responses to: www.mediatorswithoutborders.com

We value your insights.

About the Authors

Shauna Ries, L.C.S.W., M.F.T., M.D.R., President, Mediators Without Borders® and Co-Founder of InAccord Justice Centers™, Ltd.

Shauna brings an impassioned voice and vision to her role as President of Mediators Without Borders. Shauna designed the economically sustainable Center initiative and developed the empirically-tested *InAccord Conflict Analysis* Model for Alternative Dispute Resolution, in collaboration with Dr. Susan Harter. This model is based on the following InAccord Pillars: the Role of Emotions in Conflict, Empowerment, Gaining Perspective, Empathy/Compassion, and Transparency and Authenticity, as these conflict resolution principles interface with Self-Liberation. This psychologically rooted pathway is a result of over thirty years of combined work and experience as an officer in the corporate arena, leading over 600 employees and in the front lines as an Executive Vice-President, Family Clinician, Mediator and Arbitrator. This unique interdisciplinary experience enables Shauna to build bridges among diverse communities and engage in personal interactions with clarity and focus, while leading the Mediators Without Borders Organization.

Shauna is a graduate of the University of Denver where she earned a master's degree in Social Work. She completed her studies at DU with an 18 month post graduate study in Marriage and Family Therapy at the Denver Family Institute. Shauna completed post-graduate work in Mediation through a partnership program with Arcadia University International Peace and Conflict Studies Program. She is a Licensed Clinical Social Worker and worked in private practice, along with providing services for Project PAVE (Promoting Alternatives to Violence through Education) and Southern Pacific Railroad as a Mediator and Family Clinician.

In 1994, Mediators Without Borders began as RMA, a leadership, communication, stress management and conflict management organization offering individual, family and corporate training.

Shauna's initial clinical interventions involved work with couples in dispute, but subsequently expanded to deal with disputes within organizations both nationally and internationally. These early interventions were formulated into the *InAccord Conflict Analysis* Model and the *Circular Pathway to Self-Liberation.*

Shauna co-authored the book, *Quality of Life,* published by William Morrow publishing. She is a faculty member at Omega Institute in New York. Shauna is also an equestrian and rancher, residing in Boulder Colorado.

Genna Murphy, President, InAccord Justice Centers™, Ltd & Co-Founder of Mediators Without Borders®

Genna brings over twenty years of executive experience to her role as President of InAccord Justice Centers, Ltd and as Co-founder of Mediators Without Borders. Additionally, she served 18 years in private practice as a psychotherapist in Colorado and was trained in both traditional psychology as well as mind-body approaches such as Gestalt and Hakomi Therapy. Genna is a graduate of Wittenberg University and the University of Colorado Denver. She is a lifelong student, seeking what combination of behaviors and strategies work to help individuals and communities improve their quality of life. Her interest in peace building began with her involvement in the World Instant of Cooperation in December of 1986 when citizens around the world joined to meditate and reflect on bringing about a more peaceable world.

In her role as President of InAccord Justice Centers, Genna brings the fire and passion, ignited at Mediators without Borders. Genna is the lead writer of the MDR curriculum (Mediation Dispute Resolution Certificate Program), working with subject matter experts to create the materials for training Mediators and Arbitrators. Genna is the co-author of Quality of Life published by William Morrow, lead editor for *In Justice, inAccord* and the upcoming book *InAccord Conflict Analysis for Arbitrators.* Genna lives in the mountains of Colorado where she enjoys her hobbies of singing and songwriting along with hiking and skiing in the Rocky Mountains.

References

Allen, D. (2008). *Making it all work.* New York: Penguin Group.

Ardell, D. (1977). High level wellness: an alternative to doctors, drugs, and disease. Emmaus, PA: Rodale Press.

Bandura, A. (1977). *Self-efficacy: The exercise of control.* New York: Freeman Press.

Barrett-Lennard, G.T. (1981). The empathy cycle: Refinement of a nuclear concept. *Journal of Counseling Psychology, 28,* 91-100.

Batson, C. (2009). These things called empathy: Eight related but distinct phenomena. In Decety, J. & Ickes, W. (Eds.) *The social neuroscience of empathy.* Boston, MA: The Massachusetts Institute of Technology.

Bauer, J. J., & Wayment, H. A. (2008). The psychology of the quiet ego. In H.A. Wayment & J. J. Bauer (Eds.), *Transcending self-interest: Psychological explorations of the quiet ego* (pp. 7–19). Washington, DC: American Psychological Association.

Benson, H. (1975). *The relaxation response.* New York: Morrow.

Berry, J. W. (1980). Acculturation as varieties of adaptation. In A. M. Padilla (Ed.), *Acculturation Theory, models and some new findings* (pp. 9-25). Boulder, CO: Westview Press.

Berry, J. W. (2005). Acculturation. In W. Friedlmeier, P. Chakkarath, &. B. Schwartz (Eds.). *Culture and human development* (pp. 291-302). New York: Psychology Press.

Brown. K. W., & Ryan, R. M. (2003). The Benefits of Being Present: Mindfulness and Its Role in Psychological Well-Being. *Journal of Personality and Social Psychology, 84,* 822-848.

Buber, M. (1970). *I and thou.* (W. Kaufman, Trans.) New York: Charles Scribner's Sons. (Original Work published 1923).

Campbell, J. (1991). The hero's journey: Joseph Campbell on his life and work. New York: Harper & Row.

Campos, J. J., Mumme, D., Kermoian, R., & Campos, R. G. (1994). A functionalist perspective on the nature of emotions. In N. Fox (Ed.), *The development of emotion regulation* (pp. 284-303). Chicago, IL: University of Chicago Press.

Cassell, E. J. (2002). *Compassion.* In C. R. Snyder, & S. J. Lopez (Eds.), Handbook of positive Psychology (pp. 434–445). New York: Oxford University Press.

Cooper, C. R., Grotevant, H. D., & Condon, S. M. (1983). Individuality and connectedness both foster adolescent identity formation and role taking skills. In H. D. Grotevant * C. R. Cooper (Eds.), *Adolescent development in the family: New directions for child development* (pp. 43-59). San Francisco: Jossey-Bass.

Cross, S. E., & Gore, J. S. (2003). Cultural models of the self. In M. R. Leary & J. P. Tangney (Eds.), *Handbook of self and identity* (pp. 536-566). New York: Guilford Press.

Darwin, C. (1965). *The expression of the emotions in man and animals.* Chicago, IL: University of Chicago Press. (Original work published in 1872)

Deikman, A. (1982). *The observing self: Mysticism and psychotherapy.* Boston, MA: Beacon Press Books.

Elkind, D. (1967). Egocentrism in Adolescence. *Child Development Volume 38.*, 1025-1034.

Epley, N, Morewedge, C., & Boyaz, K. (2003). Perspective taking in children and adults: Equivalent egocentrism but differential correction. *Journal of Experimental Psychology, 40, 760-768.*

Exline, J.J. (2008). Taming the wild ego. In J.A. Bauer & H.A. Wayment (Eds.), Transcending self-interest: Psychological explorations of the Quiet ego (pp.53-62). Washington, DC: American Psychological Association.

Fischer, K. W. (1980). A theory of cognitive development: The control and construction of hierarchies of skills. *Psychological Review, 87,* 477-531.

Fischer, K. W., & Bidell, T. R. (2006). Dynamic development of action and thought. In W. Damon & R. M. Lerner (Eds.) & R. M. Lerner (Vol. Ed.), *Handbook of child psychology: Vol. 1. Theoretical models of human development* 6th ed., pp. 313-399). New York: Wiley.

Fischer, M., (2001). *Conflict transformation by training in nonviolent action. Activities of the Centre for Nonviolent Action (Sarajevo) in the Balkan Region.* Berghof Occasional Paper No. 18. Berlin: Berghof Research Center.

Fredrickson, B. L. (1998). What good are position emotions? *Review of General Psychology, 2,* 300-319.

Freud, S. (1952). *A general introduction to psychoanalysis.* New York: International Universities Press.

Friedman, R., & Liu, W. (2009). Bicultural in management: Leveraging the benefits of intrapersonal diversity. In R. S. Wyer, C. Chiu & Y. Hong (Eds.), *Understanding culture: Theory, research and application.* New York: Psychology Press.

Friedman, V. J. & Antal, A. B. (2005). Negotiating reality: A theory of action approach to intercultural competences. Management learning, 36 (1), 68-86.

Frijda, N. H., Manstead, A. S. R., & Bem, S. (2000). *Emotions and beliefs: How feelings influence thoughts.* Cambridge, UK: University Press.

Gibran, K. (1923). *The prophet.* New York: Alfred A. Knopf.

Gilovich, T., Epley, N., Hanko, K. (2005). Shallow thoughts about the self: The automatic components of self-assessment. In M. D. Alicke, D.. Dunning, & J. Krueger (Eds.), *The self in social judgment* (pp. 67-84). New York: Psychology Press.

Goldman, B. M. (2006). Making diamonds out of coal: The role of authenticity in healthy (optimal) self-esteem and psychological functioning. In M. H. Kernis (Ed.), *Self-esteem: Issues and answers* (pp. 132-139). New York: Psychology Press.

Goldman, B. M., & Kernis, M. H. (2002). The role of authenticity in healthy psychological functioning and subjective well-being. *Annals of the American Psychotherapy Association, 5*, 18-20.

Hahn, T.N., & Aitken, R. (1996). The Long Road Turns to Joy: A Guide to Walking Meditation. Parallax Press.

Hahn, T. N. (2013). In the country of the present moment, *Shambhala Sun, 21,* 41-49.

Hall, E.T. (1976). *Beyond culture.* New York: Random House.

Halliday, E. (1989). *Reflexive Self-Consciousness.* New York: Melchisedec Press.

Harter, S. (1999). *The construction of the self: A developmental perspective (lst ed.).* New York: Guilford Press.

Harter, S. (2012). *The construction of the self: Developmental and sociocultural foundations* (2ⁿᵈ ed.). New York: Guilford Press.

Harter, S. (2013). Emerging self-processes in childhood and adolescence. In M. Leary & J. Tangney (Eds.) *The handbook of self and identity.* New York: Guilford Press.

Harter, S., Bresnick, S., Bouchey, H. A., & Whitesell, N. R. (1997). The development of multiple role-related selves during adolescence. *Developmental Psychology, 23,* 388-399.

Hong, Y., Morris, M. W., Chiu, C., & Benet-Martinez, V. (2000). Multicultural minds: A dynamic constructivist approach to culture and cognition. *American Psychologist, 55,* 709-720.

James, W. (1890). *Principles of Psychology.* Chicago, IL: Encyclopedia Brittanica.

Kabat-Zinn, J. (1990). Full catastrophe living: Using the wisdom of your body and mind to face stress, pain and illness. New York: Delacorte.

Kabat-Zinn, J. (1994). Wherever you go, there you are: Mindfulness meditation in everyday life. New York: Hyperion.

Kabat-Zinn, J. (2003). Mindfulness-based interventions in context: Past, present, and future. Clinical Psychology: Science and Practice, 10, 144–156.

Kabat-Zinn, J. (2005). Coming to our senses. New York: Hyperion

Lama, Dalai: His holiness. (2011). *Beyond religion: Ethics for a whole world.* New York: Houghton Mifflin Harcourt.

Lama, Dalai & Cutler, H. (1998). *The art of happiness: A handbook for living.* New York: Riverhead Books.

Langer, E. (2009). *Mindfulness versus positive evaluation.* In S. J Lopez & C. R. Snyder (Eds.,*Oxford handbook of positive psychology* (2nd ed., pp. 279-294). New York: Oxford University Press.

Leary, M. (2004). *The curse of the self: Self-awareness, egotism, and the quality of human life.*Oxford, England: Oxford University Press.

Lerner, H. G. (1993). *The dance of deception.* New York: HarperCollins.

Maslow, A. (1954). *Motivation and personality.* New York: Harper & Row.

Mehta, T. (2005). *Multiple selves in South Asian adolescents.* Unpublished doctoral dissertation, University of Denver, Denver, CO.

Michie, S. & Gooty, J. (2005) Values, emotions and authenticity: Will the real leader please stand up? *Leadership Quarterly,* 16: 441-457.

Oakley, J. (1992). *Morality and the emotions.* London: Routledge.

Perls, F. (1966). *Gestalt therapy verbatim.* Gouldsboro, Minnesota: The Gestalt Journal Press, Inc.

Piaget, J. (1960). *The psychology of intelligence.* Patterson, N J: Littlefield-Adams.

Pronin, E., Puccio, C., & Ross, L. (2002). Understanding misunderstanding: Social psychological perspectives. In T. Gilovich, D. W.Griffin, & D. Kahneman (Eds.), Heuristics and biases: The psychology of intuitive judgment (pp. 636–665). Cambridge: Cambridge University Press.

Rappaport, J. (1987). Terms of empowerment/exemplars of prevention: Toward a theory for community psychology. *American Journal of Community Psychology*, 15, 121-148.

Ries, S. & Murphy, G. (1999). *Quality of Life*. New York: William Morrow and Company, Inc.

Ries, S. & Harter, S. (2012). *In Justice, InAccord*. Bradenton, FL: BookLocker.com, Inc.

Rogers, C. (1980). *A way of being*. New York: Houghton Mifflin Company.

Saarni, C., Campos, J. J., Camras, L. A., & Witherington, D. (2006). In N. Eisenberg (Vol. ed.) and in W. Damon & R. M. Lerner (editors in chief), *Handbook of child psychology, Social, emotional, and personality development* (Vol. 3, pp. 226-299). New York: Wiley.

Segal, Z.V., Williams, J.M.G., & Teasdale, J.D. (2002). *Mindfulness-based cognitive therapy for depression: A new approach to preventing relapse*. New York: Guilford Press.

Seligman, M. (1975). *Helplessness: On depression, development, and death*. San Francisco: Freeman.

Shapiro, S. L., Carlson, L. E., Astin, J. A. and Freedman, B. (2006). Mechanisms of mindfulness.*Journal of Clinical Psychology*. (Vol. 62: 373–386). New York: Wiley & Sons.

Shapiro, D.H. (1992). A preliminary study of long term meditators: Goals, effects, religious orientation, cognitions. *Journal of Transpersonal Psychology*, 24, 23–39.

Sherman, L. & Strang, H. (2007). Restorative Justice: The Evidence. Philadelphia: The Smith Institute, University of Pennsylvania.

Stotland, E. (1969). Exploratory investigations of empathy. In L. Berkowitz (ed.), *Advances in experimental social psychology* (Vol. 4, pp. 271-313). New York: Academic Press.

Tangney, J. P. (2009). Humility. In S. J. Lopez & C. R. Snyder (Eds.), *Oxford handbook of positive psychology* (2nd ed., pp. 483-490). New York: Oxford University Press.

Ting-Toomey, S., & Chung, L.C. *(2005)*. *Understanding intercultural communication.* Los Angeles, CA: Roxbury Publishing Company.

Wayment, H. A., & Bauer, J. J. (2008). *Transcending self-interest: Psychological explorations of the quiet ego.* Washington, DC: American Psychological Association.

Yang, K.S. (1995). *Indigenous psychological research in Chinese Societies.* Taiwan: Kuew Guan.